Adoption Records Handbook

Birth Family Searches
Made Easier with Self-Help
Tips, Registries, Search Angels,
Pro Se Legal Forms, etc.

Teresa [A] Brown

Crary Publications
Las Vegas, Nevada

Disclaimer
This book is written for general information purposes only and is not
intended as a substitute for legal advice nor to advocate illegal means
to obtain sealed adoption records information. You should consult an
attorney familiar with your particular situation and the laws in your
state if you have questions. Neither the author, publisher, nor any
others involved in the making of this book assumes any responsibility
for the use or misuse of information and sources contained in this
book, and specifically disclaim any liability or loss that may be
incurred as a consequence of the use and application, directly or
indirectly, of any information or contacts presented, nor liability or
responsibility for inadvertent errors or omissions. Readers accept all
information herein without warranty, express or implied. Any slights
of people, places, or groups are unintentional.

Edited by Lisa Caza of Free Spirit Literary

Publisher's Cataloging-In-Publication Data
Brown, T. A. (Teresa A.)
 Adoption records handbook : birth family searches made easier with self-
help tips, registries, search angels, pro se legal forms, etc./ T.A. Brown.

 p. : forms ; cm.

Includes index.
 ISBN 978-0-9743438-6-0

1. Birthparents--United States--
Identification--Handbooks, manuals, etc. 2. Adoptees--United States. 3.
Adoption--Law and legislation--United States--Handbooks, manuals, etc.
4. Adoption--Law and legislation--United States--Forms. I. Title.

HV875.55 .B76 2008
362.82/98

                                                      2008906411

Crary Publications
405 Lehman Street
Las Vegas, Nevada 89110

Dedicated to adoptees and birth families
everywhere who are in search of each other.
Let them find their answers and be at peace.

"I am only one, but I am one. I cannot do everything, but I can do something. And I will not let what I cannot do interfere with what I can do." —Edward Everett Hale

Table of Contents

Civil Right

It is a civil right of all citizens to be able to obtain the original government documents of their birth.

A civil right, by its very nature, cannot be compromised. A civil right belongs equally to all members of a society.

- The Fourteenth Amendment to the U. S. Constitution states: "No state shall make or enforce any law which shall abridge the privileges or immunities of citizens of the United States, nor shall any state deprive any person of life, liberty, or property, without due process of law, nor deny to any person within its jurisdiction the equal protection of its laws."
- It is unjust for any state or country to single out one group of adult citizens by the passage of laws that serve to conceal the true circumstances of their births. All non-adopted citizens of the United States and Canada may request and receive original birth documents under clear statutory procedure.
- It is unjust to deny a right to a group of citizens based on what they "might" do if they were restored that right.
- It is unjust to violate adult adoptees' rights to privacy from government interference in their personal lives.
- It is unjust for the government to regulate an adult adoptees' personal choice to associate with his or her birth family. The government does not regulate the personal choices of any other groups of citizens to freely associate with one another.
- It is unjust for our laws and policies to deprive one group of their rights in order to protect others from possibly having to face the consequences of their past choices.
- It is unjust for a state to uphold a promise made between private citizens, especially when a third party's rights are taken away by such a promise.

- It is unjust to allow any parents to have a lifetime control over the information contained in their children's original birth certificate. This information belongs to the person whose history it records - the adoptee. It does NOT belong to that person's parents.

The Civil Right statement above was obtained with permission from www.Bastards.org

An except from Leviticus 25:10 on the Liberty Bell says, "And ye shall hallow the fiftieth year, and proclaim liberty through-out all the land unto all the inhabitants thereof: it shall be a jubilee unto you; and ye shall return every man unto his possession, and ye shall return every man unto his family. "

An estimated 1 in 10 Americans are adopted, and at least as many more Americans have an adoption in their immediate family.

Definition of "immediate family": one's grandparents, parents, brothers, sisters, spouse, children and grandchildren. —*The Family History Center, Church of Jesus Christ of Latter Day Saints; reprinted in "Dear Abby," Los Angeles Times, 5-30-92.*

If this book is helpful to you in finding your birth family we would love to hear about it. Send us a letter telling your story and *with your permission only,* we could post it on the website. Write or email: tabrown@crarypublications.com

If you find this book helpful, a review at Amazon.com will help others who are searching as well.

Introduction

All of the information and forms in this book are being made available to help birth families find each other and for members of the adoption triad who can't afford an attorney. You should have Microsoft Word or another Word program for these forms.

With these form templates, you can type up your own legal documents, file them "Pro Se," and submit them to the proper agency or court of record. Pro Se means, "doing it yourself." Some judges do not like Pro Se petitioners and may insist you hire an attorney, but most judges understand in adoption records cases.

In order to use these forms you will first need to find out where to file them. For example, do you file them with the state registrar, Department of Health Vital Statistics Division (addresses are listed in the back of this book), courthouse, adoption agency, or the attorney who handled your adoption? However, the most common place would be with the agency or attorney who initially handled the adoption (with the exception of the Petition; which is to be filed with the court of record). The court that has your file will be the court that finalized the adoption and the court of record. For state-by-state adoption laws, statutes, age requirements, etc. check online at: www.childwelfare.gov/systemwide/laws_policies/statutes/i nfoaccessapall.pdf.

You must be at least 18 years old to file any of these documents, and up to 21 in some states. Please note that the statutes listed in this book are not the same as the ones on the above website. Instead they are statutes that state "for good cause showing" which almost all courts require in a Petition to open adoption records.

IMPORTANT: Even if you already have your Waiver or Non-Id, please read all the instructions for each document. Some of those instructions may apply to a later document.

Remember that when you type out your own legal documents, they will look different than they do in this book. Your page size will widen, you will have more space than what is used here, your lines will not take up as much space, and your pages will be shorter. So be sure to adjust your pages accordingly. Also, keep in mind that your signature line must always be at least two lines from the previous paragraph above the date in order to be on the same page. This format is for *ALL* legal documents. Some things may be repeated throughout this book for emphasis and importance as well.

If you don't think that you can do this yourself and feel that you may need assistance, please contact your state's Bar Association and ask for names and contact information for attorneys specializing in adoption law. This book is not meant to replace an attorney, but only to help those who can't afford to pay $300 or more an hour for an attorney's time. Every second an attorney spends talking on the phone, every letter an attorney writes, and every minute an attorney spends working on your case or talking to you about the weather, your family, or your problems, *you will be billed for it.* Plan ahead for this contingency. If you can afford it, hiring an attorney is the best course of action for you when working with legal documents.

Getting Started

NECESSARY EARLY STEPS TO TAKE

There are certain steps to follow when trying to obtain information from your sealed adoption records. The most important of these steps are as follows:

1. The first and absolutely most significant thing you can do is to register with the International Soundex Reunion Registry or ISRR. Their new location is: P.O. Box 371179, Las Vegas, NV 89137. By phone call (775) 882-7755 or 888-886-ISRR. You need to be 18 to register. This is the oldest and largest free reunion registry in the world (but donations are accepted). The ISRR is a confidential, non-profit mutual consent registry dedicated to reuniting adult family members separated by adoption, divorce, or other dislocation. It is the most likely place to find a match if anyone in your birth family has also registered. However, please take note that while your registration is in fact free, they do NOT accept applications via the internet! The registration form can be printed out from their official website at: www.isrr.net and filled in afterwards in order to send it via snail mail to the above address. Also, rest assured that all information sent to the ISRR will not be given to any third party or used to solicit business for professional searchers. If you are already registered, you should call the above phone number in order to update your contact information (if it has changed).

Also register at www.registry.adoption.com and the Registry in the state you were born in. These three Registration organizations are the most likely places that could possibly yield you an immediate match. If they don't, go to the next step.

2. Send a Waiver of Confidentiality first to The Department of Health, then to the adoption agency, state records agency, and/or the attorney who handled your adoption. If your birth family also filed a Waiver of Confidentiality, this should give you your birth record information in most states.

3. Send a letter requesting Non-Identifying information to The Department of Health, adoption agency, state records agency, and/or the attorney who handled your adoption. Most states will supply you with non-identifying information at the very least. The addresses for vital records by state can be found in the back of this book.

4. Send a request letter to the Department of Health Vital Records for your original birth certificate. If they refuse, ask for the court of jurisdiction where your adoption took place so that you can Petition the court to open your records.

5. If none of the above steps produces your information after you have waited the length of time often determined by state law, you can file a Petition with the Court where your adoption was finalized in order to request an original birth certificate.

The Petition is a legal document that you can do *Pro Se* (by yourself) and that you will take to the courthouse of record to request opening your own sealed adoption records.

A few states require only an Affidavit to request birth record information. If that is the case in your state, the Affidavit and Order are included in this book. Once again, it is important to stress that these are legal documents—*you must read the directions carefully.*

These forms have been formatted for adoptees to use while in search of their birth parents information. However, a birth parent searching for a birth child can also use the forms as templates and modify them to their own use.

An important thing for all searchers to remember is to always keep copies of every form, document, or written communication you submit to anyone in your search efforts. As with any of your valuable papers (insurance, titles, deeds, birth certificates, etc.), putting an extra set of copies in a large envelope to leave with a friend, family member, or originals in a safe deposit box is prudent in case of fire.

STATES THAT HAVE OPEN ADOPTION RECORDS

As an adult adoptee, Alabama, Alaska, Deleware adoptees over the age of 21 can phone 302-739-4721 to request an application for their original birth certificate, Indiana prior to 1940, Kansas, Maine beginning in 2009, Massachusetts prior to 4/14/1974, Michigan will allow an adopted person to get a copy of his or her original birth certificate upon reaching age 21, Montana for adoptions finalized prior to 2/2/1964, New Hampshire, New Jersey prior to 1940, Ohio adoption records are open for adoptions finalized prior to 1/1/1964, Oregon, and Tennessee will provide you with an uncertified copy of your original birth certificate but no-contact veto's are available to birth parents for adoptions finalized after 1951. North Carolina has passed a bill allowing Confidential Intermediaries to act as a third party to facilitate contact.

New York provides free forms from Family Court Forms 26A through 27E at: www.courts.state.ny.us/forms/familycourt/ adoption.shtml Information can also be disclosed to adult adoptees that were born and adopted in New York through the Adoption Information Register, which is operated by the State Department of Health. In addition, birth parents can use the registry to find their children and a sibling can use the registry to find their birth sibling(s). If the counties won't accept those forms, you will most likely need to file a Petition to get a Court Order.

Occasionally a state will require a Motion rather than a Petition. We do not provide this document, but a sample of the Washington D.C. Motion and accompanying documents are found on Monique's Web Site at: www.home.comcast.net/ ~monique.jones/adoptee/DCpetition.html. Wyoming also requires a Motion and Affidavit to open adoption records as per Wyoming Statutes § 1-22-203(b).

Laws change on a yearly basis so more states may begin opening sealed adoption records as time goes by. If the above information changes or is inaccurate, please check your state for the correct information.

Off Topic Notation:

Warning to men wanting to prevent the loss of any decisions involving their birth child in the State of Utah. You must legally register a commencement of paternity with the Office of Vital Statistics in Utah within twenty-four hours of the baby's birth. After that the birth mother retains all rights to the placement of the child.

Checklist Essentials

Make yourself a basic list of facts (as seen below). Fill in as many blanks as you can and put it on the first page of your Search Journal referenced in the Tips section following this one. When you have done this, follow up by working on the checklist. Just know that the search is a long slow process for most people and it is easy to get discouraged. While you are waiting for information think of other ways you could be searching (look in the tips section for ideas) and then live your life to its fullest. Live just as you would if you were not searching. Keep busy!

Fill in everything you know to get you started. This list will help you gather the information you need.

Name:
City:
County:
State:
Country:
Birth Date:
Male or Female:
Adoptive Mother's Name:
Adoptive Mother's Maiden Name:
Adoptive Father's Name:
Birth Name:
Birth City:
Birth County:
Birth State:
Birth Country:
Birth Mother's Name:
Birth Mother's Maiden Name:
Birth Father's Name:
Birth Hospital:
Adoption Agency or Attorney:
City adoption took place:
County adoption took place:
State adoption took place:

Country adoption took place:
Searching For:

1. Create a Search Journal/Workbook.
2. Discuss the search with your family and ask for their help. If they will not help don't get discouraged or upset with them, just move on without their help. Snooping secretly in files, storage boxes or attics is always an option if the opportunity arises. Ask other relatives such as aunts, uncles, older cousins, grandparents, etc.
3. Locate your amended birth certificate.
4. Find a copy of your final adoption decree.
5. Contact the doctor listed on your birth certificate and see if he has your original birth records.
6. If you have names, check both county and state records for marriages, deaths, or divorces for both of your birth parents and birth grandparents.
7. Check your state laws.
8. Do your locations research from the libraries in the area of your birth or birth child if you can. They will have the old phone books and old local newspapers you need. Search Angels can help with this if you are not able to go yourself. See the Search Angel section in this book for a list of available Search Angels.
9. Look in the old newspapers for wedding or engagement announcements of your birth parents and for adoption notices.
10. Get your information into adoption search magazines.
11. If you are unable to do out-of-town research personally, hire a local researcher to do it for you or check our list of search angels to see if there are any in your area of research.
12. Get a few business cards made up with your name, address, phone number and search email address on them.
13. Read the Tips section that follows for more detailed help.

Search Tips

To begin with, it is prudent to remember that there will always be opposition and closed doors towards anyone searching for their birth family. It is best to come up with a plausible story that has nothing to do with adoption. Lost family members, genealogical searches, college roommates of your parents, family death notifications, etc. are all possibilities. Keep it simple and geared to the situation. Genealogy research seems to be the most common one used. In addition, if you have to make many phone calls during your search and need to use 411 information for the numbers, dial 1-800-FREE411 and you will not be charged for the information request.

If your search has you frustrated, upset, or angry, do not let it show. Always be kind and humble to those you are asking for help, even if they do not give you the information you need. They may remember you later and return your kind attitude unexpectedly.

Address Changes

If you should move and you have registered with the I.S.R.R. or on any other registries, please update your information. If a match is made and they cannot locate you, you have lost what you are searching for. Search Angels say the most frustrating part of trying to help people is when they lose a match because they no longer have a current address for the person they are helping. Please, always update your location!

To find someone who has moved, send mail addressed to him or her to the old address. In bold letters write ADDRESS CORRECTION REQUESTED, DO NOT FORWARD, and if that does not produce results, resend and add, "Please check expired files and refer to carrier if necessary."

Another address or "additional" address you might seriously consider for yourself is a post office box to weed out any nuts who may try to contact you. Get an anonymous free email address at Yahoo, Google, or AOL outside of your regular email address and use it strictly for adoption related information. This will give you another layer of protection if your ISP fails you, you change ISPs, or your computer crashes. You can still retrieve mail from this other service while also maintaining your privacy.

Adoption Agencies & Attorneys

Whenever possible contact the adoption agency as well as the attorney who handled your adoption either in person or by phone. Personal appointments are the best for building rapport and could give the person you are talking to the chance to leave the room with your file in sight. There is also the chance that they could off-handedly mention some valuable information. The worst that could happen is you may be charged for the visit.

When you request non-id ask for a photocopy as opposed to a summary. A busy employee generally retypes summaries and may leave out important details, while a photocopy can give clues on where to search next. You can often figure out how many letters of the alphabet have been whited (or blacked) out by lining the line up to the next one that hasn't been whited out. If you know how many digits are covered up in the state, you'll know how many letters are contained in the city. This will help narrow your search. Expect fees for these services.

If you don't know the name of the attorney or the adoption agency the following letter example will help you request that information from the Vital Statistics Bureau.

Date

Bureau of Vital Statistics
Street Address
City, State and Zip

Re: Locating Adoption Agency or Attorney

To Whom It May Concern:

I would like to request your help in locating the Adoption Agency or Attorney that handled my adoption. Can you please send me any information you have on either the agency or attorney and how I can contact them?

Enclosed is a copy of my amended birth certificate to help you locate my file, along with a self-addressed-stamped-envelope for your reply.

I appreciate your time and effort and I look forward to hearing back from you at your earliest convenience. If you have any questions and need to contact me, my information is below. Thank you.

Respectfully,

Your written signature

YOUR Typed NAME
Your Street
Your City, State and zip
Your phone number
Your email address if you have one

AOL

If you are a member of AOL and have a name to search with then you have access to a vast amount of profiles that list where people come from as well as their age. If you have a name or just a town and an approximate year, you can find people from the same town who may know the birth family member you are looking for, or who are willing to look up a name in the phone book or an old high school yearbook. Most people are kind and are happy to help others find lost relatives for genealogical information, or find old school family friends.

If you do not have a name, see if you can find classmates who might have information about someone who left school before the end of the term. Be discrete. One woman IM's them and often gets them to look up her information while she's talking to them, and if she can't do that, she emails them.

Birth Certificate Codes

When an Amended Birth Certificate is issued by the court in charge, they usually do not change the vital information or else they can alter it entirely. If you want to validate your place of birth on the Amended Birth Certificate, check the following codes. However, not all states adhere to the Federal Codes. New Hampshire, Maryland, New York, and Pennsylvania are some of them.

The first digit on your birth certificate number is a 1 that signifies you were born in the United States. The second two digits signify the state where you were born. The fourth and fifth digits on all birth certificates, amended and original, signify the year you were born. The following codes show the state of birth.

AK – 50	AL – 01	AR – 03	AZ – 02	CA – 04
CO – 05	CT – 06	DC – 08	DE – 07	FL – 09
GA – 10	HI – 51	IA – 14	ID – 11	IL – 12
IN – 13	KS – 15	KY – 16	LA – 17 or 57	
MA – 20	MD – 19 or 54		ME – 18	MI – 21
MN – 22	MO – 24	MS – 23	MT – 25	NC – 32
ND – 33	NE – 26	NH – 28	NJ – 29	NM – 30
NV – 27	NY – 31 or 56		OH – 34	OK – 35
OR – 36	PA – 137	RI – 38	SC – 39	SD – 40
TN – 41	TX – 42	UT – 44	VA – 45	VT – 43
WA – 46	WI – 48	WV – 47	WY – 49	

In many states an adopted child's birth certificate is only amended and the original number on the birth certificate remains the same. If you have a strong and patient desire to search you can take the book with birth records from the year you were born and search through all the pages until you find the number that matches your birth certificate. This is time consuming but it produced results for one lady and she found her birth parents names as well as her own birth name.

Catholic Charities & Church Records

If your adoption was through Catholic Charities and you would like to find out what services are available for you, contact their office in the city where your adoption took place. If you do not know, write to their main office at:

Catholic Charities USA
National Headquarters
1731 King St, Alexandria, VA 22314
(703) 549-1390

Often babies given up through Catholic Charities were baptized before being adopted out. If Catholic or other church baptism records are available, babies born on your birth date and baptized in a parish or church in the city you were born in could be a possible source for your original birth name. For older children who were adopted out of an orphanage there may even be information on your first communion record.

Ask to see the ledgers of baptism to see if you are listed. Just don't mention you were adopted when you ask to see if you were baptized within a short time after your birth. It is said that the birth name is crossed off and replaced with the adopted name although this has not been verified for the purpose of this publication.

If you receive your non-id information from Catholic Charities, look for anything that is highlighted on older records. Sympathetic nuns used to highlight true facts including a first name of a birth parent or child.

As a rule, all churches keep excellent records so if your birth family was religious, then these records would be worth digging deeper into without mentioning the word *adoption*. Check all churches in the area of your adoption. If you can find a friendly church member through their women's group, someone may very well be willing to volunteer to look for you if you cannot do it yourself.

City & County Archives

In your search for old records, begin with the town and county areas where you were born or where your adoption was filed. The local archives may contain information unavailable anywhere else. After that, check the state archives. A list of state archives is found at the end of this book.

City Directories

From the mid-1800s to the present day, most cities and counties have produced city directories (sometimes called farmers' directories or business directories). In some towns, they even listed the children and their occupations (remember that in the early to mid-1900s, most folks did not have the privilege of graduating from high school, let alone attend college). It is not unusual to find 15-year-old boys listed in city directories with "laborer" or "tinsmith." In addition, the directory might list children and say "student," which would indicate that they were still in high school or college.

You can actually track a family throughout the years, showing addresses, occupations (even sometimes, where they actually worked — factory, shipyard, etc.). It also might show members of extended families who moved in and out of the home over the years. Old employers can be a good resource as well and former landlords who may have a forwarding address.

Start at the year you know the family lived at a certain address and begin working backward. Then come back and work forward. Don't give up if you find some unlisted years — it might just mean that they missed sending the forms back or they weren't at home when the enumerator called. There was no charge to be listed in the directory, but no compulsion, either; it was not mandatory like the census. Compare these findings to the phone book, but remember that it wasn't until the mid-'50s or '60s that most folks had telephones, so don't be surprised if they aren't listed earlier.

When you have established what neighborhood(s) the family lived in, look for the appropriate schools. Go find the yearbooks (usually housed in one major library in town — call around and ask) and look up pictures and more information about the family's children — even the brothers and sisters of your birth parents. You may be able to find them through these siblings. Old neighbors are excellent sources of information as well. They may very well keep in touch with your birth family or know of their friends. Go visit them in person if you can for much better responses.

If you can establish when the birth grandparents died, you can look up obituaries; obtain death certificates, or funeral home or cemetery records. These documents would give the decedent's next of kin and the "informant" — usually a spouse or a child — with their address. If an estate was filed, you can look in the county Surrogate Court records (in NY State; Probate Courts in most other states). That will show all heirs and their addresses as of the time the will was filed for probate.

Many of these directories have "reverse address" listings. If you only have an address, you can go to the alphabetical listing for the town, search for 123, and get not only who lived at that address, but also all the neighbors up and down the street.

Call the local library and ask them to check the city directory for the year that person was born, plus the years before and after. You can have them check by the address, then go to the alphabetical listing and see what else you can find.

Here are some online links that will help you in your quest:
Effective use of City Directories:
www.progenealogists.com/citydirectories.htm
Inventory of CrissCross Directories & Street Address Directories:
www.loc.gov/rr/business/directories/crisscross.html
City directories are listed alphabetically nationwide. Posted by the Library of Congress: www.distantcousin.com/Directories/

CIs & Independent Search Consultants

Confidential Intermediaries (CIs) are court appointed. If you wish to independently hire a CI please check them out first and get references. There have been some negative reports so make sure you find a reputable CI before committing yourself.

An expensive option is an Independent Search Consultant (ISC). They are certified through extensive testing and considered to be the best money can buy. The more information you have, the quicker your results. If you can afford to hire an ISC it might be your best option.

Court Records Retrievals

Old court transcripts of hearings on parental rights being relinquished used to be public records and could be found in the county of birth or at the State Archives. These transcripts would give names and addresses and other adoption information.

This requires a bit more work to locate since you will need to locate the court docket number first and then to the court book that contain the court orders. If you know the name of the agency that handled the adoption, the court dockets usually list the agency which would make it easier for you to locate.

Name Change documents may have been filed with the court by your adoptive parents if your adoption had not gone through right away after they took you home. Most likely, your original name was something like "Baby Doe," only with your birth mother's last name on it. The name change document would give you your birth last name if nothing else.

If you can not do the research yourself or find a search angel to do it for you, Research and Retrieval (800-707-8771) has experienced researchers in virtually every court in the nation. They will not only do court records, but almost any kind of publicly available document retrieval you need: library archives, any government agency, anything on paper or film.

They are very reasonable in price and they will do your run usually the same day or 2-3 at the most. What is encouraging is that they are also used by many PIs. Their website is: www.researchandretrieval.com

Deceased Adoptive Parents

If either of your adoptive parents is deceased, you might try checking with the friends in the book people signed when paying their respects. If your adoptive mom belonged to any women's groups in her church, someone there may have information or names. The funeral home may also have a name not listed in the visitors book. Give them a call.

Extracting ID Information

First, photocopy your non-id information. Try a color copy, then black and white, and finally red (yes, red), and you might be surprised what shows through. Secondly, by process of elimination, read the paper (s) and see where there may be duplicates of the same word. Example: "Miss Doe" or "Miss Doe's". Keep in mind that you may be able to line up letters and get a "count" of them by what's above and underneath. Don't forget to count spaces too. Typewriters have a fixed font width so letters remain the same consistently.

"Joe" obtained a copy of his Final Decree of Adoption from the court clerk where his adoption was finalized. He simply asked, paid a small fee, and it was given to him. Just before the clerk handed it to him, she took a marker and blackened out his birth name and his birth parents names. Joe took his copy home and used hair spray and cologne (sparingly) on the document and managed to lift the black marker from enough of the letters to be able to find the names that were covered. If this document had been photocopied *after* it was blackened, it would not have worked, but another copy from a different clerk at a different time might not be photocopied after the marker is applied.

Always keep a couple of copies untouched so you can run them to the local tanning bed and possibly read through. "Natural light" light bulbs (full spectrum or plant lights) have also been found to expose a great deal. Letters have actually been confirmed this way.

Always make sure you find a spot to test on the document before you do the whole thing. It will save you having to get another copy of the court documents.

If the black marker used on your document was a sharpie, it will come off with a little isopropanal (rubbing alcohol). Do it very carefully. Practice on other copies so you don't ruin the good copy. Using a Q-Tip works best. Use at least 70% ethanol, but 100% works the best. If it wasn't a sharpie or another brand that uses the same kind of ink, but still a marker, it was probably more like a laundry pen. That kind of ink comes off with a little acetone. Nail polish remover and hair spray will also remove most inks.

Sometimes if you just lay the paper against another blank piece and rub across the marked part with a dime or something the letters show up on the blank sheet, Most of this stuff only works if the marker is on an original—not a copy—of a marked page.

Historical Societies

Here you can find county histories, old newspapers records, census rolls, and telephone directories. You could also find old records of hospitals, children's homes, utility companies, hospitals, etc.

Hospitals & Doctors

If the doctor or obstetrician that delivered you is listed on your amended birth certificate or you know who he or she is, make an appointment if you live in the same area or write a letter. Some (but not all) doctors tend to keep their old records.

If you are a birthparent searching, the name of who paid your doctor's bill could provide the adopted parent's name. The doctor's or hospital's billing department may have that record in their archives or on microfiche.

If you are an adoptee, find out if the hospital where you were born kept birth journals or obgyn logs from the Delivery Room clerk. Give them the date of birth and ask for the information on baby boy/girl and the last name if you know it. This may give you some non-identifying information.

Also, go to the Medical Records Department. Your admission card may be there with the name of your birth mother on it. If they say they no longer have the complete hospital records, request to see a copy of the Index card. Once again, do not mention the word adoption in any of your search efforts if you want to find anything out.

If you are not snooping personally and you are not able to go to the hospital, but instead decide to write a letter, you will not be able to hide the fact that you were adopted. Following is a sample letter of what you might write if you know the name or surname you were given at birth. To make the letter personal (they might appreciate your effort), call the hospital operator and ask for the name of the Hospital Administrator, but do not ask to talk to them. Just get the name for your letter. Do not italicize anything in your letter.

Date

Hospital Administrator (name if you know it)
Hospital Name
Street Address
City, State and Zip
To Whom It May Concern *(or,* Dear *their name):*

I would like to request copies of archived or microfiche patient files from the date of my birth on (date of your birth) under the name of Baby (boy or girl) (name here) *Doe.* Enclosed is a $20 money order made out to your hospital, which should cover the cost of copies and postage.

Can you please send me copies of as much of the following that is available?

Full name of patient
Medical history of patient if available
Address of patient
Marital status
Next of kin
Admission papers
Who paid the bill
Delivery Doctor's name *(if you don't have it)*
Birth records, including footprint if available
Obgyn records
Maternity ward index card
Nursery records
Time of birth

I look forward to hearing back from you at your earliest convenience. Thank you.

Respectfully,

Your written signature

YOUR Typed NAME
Your Street
Your City, State and zip
Your phone number
Your email address if you have one

Journal

When you start your journal (preferably one with pockets for documents) make copies of everything you put in it, including notes. Put all of it in a large manila envelope and keep it somewhere safe in case of fire (this has actually happened), theft, or loss of some kind. Keep the copied records updated regularly the same as you do the original copy. Put the second copy somewhere other than your home or leave it with someone you trust.

Write down every group and registry that you have posted on and be sure to check back often. Always date everything and keep track of every person you have contacted and the results of that contact. Make sure to update each group and registry if you should move, change your email address, or change any other information. They can't help you or connect you to your birth family if they can't find you.

LDS Records

"Kendall," having been told by her doctor that the adoptive parents were LDS, went to the LDS Genealogical Library in Salt Lake City, took two volumes from the archives with the surname she remembered seeing when she signed the private relinquishment papers and started searching. For no particular reason she opened the first volume right in the middle, turned a page and the family record was right in front of her. She found out what name they had given the baby and there was an old address as a starting point. This led to a reunion.

LDS Family History Centers also have many genealogy records that you can view at centers nationwide. You can order films sent to your local center for a very small fee and they will hold it there for you for two months. They will not search for you, but they will be there to help you use their equipment and direct you to the records you wish to research. Be discreet and do not mention adoption searching. It is best to say that you are doing research for genealogical purposes. This is the truth!

Legal Notices

There are two different types of legal notices that can be found in the classified section of newspapers that relate to adoptions. These notices are required by law in some states, but not all unfortunately, and are simply legal notices for interested parties. If the adoption took place in two different states or counties, check in both county newspapers as well as any other newspapers in both areas.

The first is the "notice of adoption," often called a "citation of adoption." This normally includes the birth name of the adoptee as "baby boy or girl" followed by the birth mother's last name. It will also list the full names of the adoptive parents. In 1946 Arizona, both birth parents full names and state of residence was listed. This information would help a birth parent searching for a relinquished adult child as well as the reverse.

The second type of legal notice is a "termination of parental rights proceeding" or "abandonment citation." These generally reveal the birth name of the adoptee as well as the full names of the birth parents.

Libraries Where Baby Was Born

Ask all the libraries librarian's to check for the name in newspapers during that time frame and even go back and forward a couple of years either way. That name could be either your birthmother's maiden name or your birthfather's surname so check all possible leads with that in mind.

Libraries can also house old local telephone books and newspapers. Ask the librarian in the city of the baby's birth in if they can do a search in their database for the name you are searching for. It could lead to family members who may still live in the area.

Mail Forwarding

California has an excellent service whereby they will forward a letter to someone if a person writes to the DMV and asks for a letter to be forwarded. States that provide this service will charge a small fee. The minimal information you need will be a name and year/date of birth. It works the same way as the Social Security Administration's letter forwarding service. If this service does not currently exist where you live, petition your state to implement California's letter forwarding service through its Driver's License Division.

The address for SS mail forwarding is at: Social Security Administration Location Services, 6401 Security Blvd., Baltimore, Maryland 21235. They will forward only if given a specific reason such as for medical reasons. As usual, do not mention adoption or adoption related topics.

Maternity Homes

The Catholic Charities homes for unwed mothers, Booth Maternity homes, Edna Gladney Home for Unwed Mothers, and St. Agnes Maternity Home are often interchangeable with second chance homes. A list of closed Maternity Homes is online along with the locations of where some of the records are at: members.aol.com/afresources/frc/other/maternity.html *Information taken from the Salvation Army Website:* If you are interested in obtaining information regarding the Salvation Army Maternity Home and Hospital Records, please email Lois.Sellars@usw.salvationarmy.org, or call our toll free number 1-800-698-7728, Monday-Friday, 8:30 a.m. to noon and 1:00 p.m. to 4:00 p.m. Pacific Time and ask for Booth records. A form will be sent to you for notarization. This form must be on file before any acknowledgement of records is given. A processing fee may be charged.

MySpace & Yahoo

Some birth families have found each other in Groups found at MySpace, Yahoo, Facebook and others. Join them all, or at least the most populated few and search for any groups that have to do with the keywords: adoption, adoptees, birth family, birth moms, reunions, birth family searches, and any others you can think of that has to do with adoption. For Yahoo you just need to sign up for their free email account which you should have as an anonymous email for your adoption related searches anyway. Then go to "Groups" on their website and start searching. In MySpace go to: Groups, Family & Home, and then type Adoption in their Search Groups box on the right hand side. In Facebook type "Adoptees" in the search box and then select "Common Interest Families."

Use a signature line whenever and wherever you post that lists your name, birth date, birthplace, and names of any birth family members if you have them.

Newspapers

If you are lucky enough to have a name or a place of birth, you could place an ad in the major local newspaper from where you are searching. One woman did it on a weekly basis and found her birth siblings this way. You might even find an ad placed by your birth family member searching for you. The most common place to advertise as well as find these ads is under Personals in the Classifieds section of the paper. Also place ads in the online classifieds section of newspapers in the region where you are searching.

Your ad might read: Missing Person, Birthmother of Baby Doe (your birth last name here if you know it) born (your birth date) in (hospital) (city, state). Reply to: (Your Post Office Box number preferably, or your address.)

Many years ago, newspapers used to post adoption notices in the classified section of the newspapers. This notice lists the names of both birth parents and where they resided at the time of the adoption. The notice would have been posted in the newspaper located where the adoption took place. Call the court clerk where your adoption took place and ask what newspaper they publish their legal notices in.

There is always the slim chance that a birth announcement was put in your birth town's newspaper. I would also recommend searching for birth announcements in the town/city where your adoptive parents resided at the time of your birth. There are many cases in which adoptive parents lived in a completely different town than that of the adoptee's – some parents may have announced the baby's birth in *their* area – as they would be, much like many other parents, very proud and wish to announce their child's arrival.

If you know the date and time of your birth, start checking from the day you were born to at least a week after. Illegitimate births were not published until the late 70's.

Another idea is to write down a list of all the information from the babies born three days before and three days after your birth. This will give you a list of the names of all the families who would have been in the hospital at the same time as your birth mother and one of them may have met her or even been her roommate. Gossip from any of them may produce results. If you are a birth parent searching, someone on that list may be friends of the adopting parents or remember being at the baby window with the adopting family and struck up a conversation with them. Gossip can yield more clues to add to your list.

Before you set out on your quest to find these people from the hospital, it would be helpful to you to get some blank business cards from your local office supplies store. Put your name, phone number and email address on them along with your birth date and place and name of who you are searching for if you know it, so you can hand them to the people you talk to in case they or one of their family members remember something important later on.

To find the people on your list go to the online people searches and phone each and every one of them. You can also go to their last known addresses and ask the person who lives there now as well as their neighbors on both sides of the street if they know where the people moved to. Tell him or her a condensed version of your story without being overly assertive and then leave your card so they can contact you later if they obtain information from another family member.

Don't forget to try the small town newspapers. The following website archives small town newspapers dating back to 1865. www239.smalltownpapers.com/smalltownpapers/jsp/stphome.jsp

Obituaries

There is a wealth of information in obituaries. If you have a name and the birth parent you are looking for is deceased, the obituary will list survivors and will tell you where their children (your siblings) were at the time of death as well as list the married names of your sisters if you have any. If you have a death certificate but are unable to locate an obituary, try calling the funeral home listed on the death certificate. They may be able to provide you with a copy of the obituary or list of the survivors. If not, go to the library of the town where the death occurred and ask the librarian if the newspapers for their town are indexed on their computers. If they are, input the name in their database and it will search and find that persons name every time it is mentioned. Also, input any other family member names you may have.

Odds 'n Ends

- Falsified birth certificates, data and samples can be found at www.peoplefindernow.com/3adofals.htm
- Wills are likely to clarify relationships.
- Under the relationships column in census records the letters AD before daughter or son indicates an adopted child.
- There will be people who use nick-names rather than their given name. This website may help: www.whatsinaname.net/
- See if your library has a book called "Adoption, Orphanages, Maternity Homes: An Historical Directory" by Reg Niles. It lists nationwide institutions in existence up to 1981, which includes addresses and other valuable information. Also put the name of the institution into your search engine to try to locate the archived records.
- Write to the Adoption Regulation Unit in your state to request your adoption records.

Old Search Websites

Have you ever gone to that web site looking for more genealogy information only to find it is not there any more? This is where old web sites go to die. Therefore, if you are looking for a web site that no longer exists you can try the WayBackMachine at: www.archive.org. They may not have everything but it never hurts to look.

Old Yearbooks

Many birth parents have been found in old high school yearbooks. If you know the name you were given before your adoption, your original last name is something to search for in high school yearbooks (in the state you were born in). Alumni location records may also be available. The following website has a list of people who have access to certain yearbooks who are willing to look up names for searchers at: www. gsadoption registry.com/searchangels/gsangelsyearbooks.html   Another resource is Alumni Find, a free service to find old classmates. Your birth family member just may have registered. www.alumni-find.com. Something that some adoptees have started doing is registering themselves as a "student" with their birth name and the maternity home their first mother stayed at.

Passport Information

In order to find out when a person enters or leaves the country, write a Freedom of Information Act request to U.S. Customs for the Customs Declaration Forms that people have to sign when coming back from abroad. They are public records.

Phone Books

If you have a name, the most often overlooked idea is to look in the phone books where you think your birth family might be. Another idea that worked for one person is to list yourself in the phone book in the town where you or your child was born should they look for you there and list it under the name you went by when your baby was born.

You will also want to list yourself in the major internet "phone books" such as: 411, 555-1212, Switchboard, Yahoo's People Search, Google, Infoseek, Infospace, AnyWho.com, WhoWhere .com, Four11, and Bigfoot.

Railroads

Old railroad employees' social security numbers were all changed to a 700 - 728 prefix number. Therefore, if you find any social security numbers beginning with 700 - 728, you will know that they worked for the railroad. However, please note that this practice was discontinued somewhere around the 1960's.

RegDay

The month of November is the national Registration Day, an annual event to increase public awareness of the International Soundex Reunion Registry (ISRR – please see the Getting Started section of this book for further information regarding this agency). Volunteer your time to help set up a table in front of a busy store if at all possible. Barnes & Noble and Borders have sponsored RegDay and will also let you do this, but more traffic runs through a store such as Wal-Mart where many a successful registration day has taken place. You can also get free publicity for this event through newspapers and radio stations.

By volunteering your time, you will be networking and helping others that in turn could come back and help you. RegDay's official website is www.regday.org. Check out their website in September so that you will have plenty of time to find a place to sponsor a table and get the supplies you need.

Search Letter - Generic

Mail a letter/flyer to every person in the city (and the smaller outlying areas if you can) of your birth family's last known location. "Mindy" found her birth parents from an old newspaper clipping in Phoenix on her adoption that listed not only both of her birth parents full names but where they were from as well. She was able to track down her birth mother's family and her siblings by sending copies of a letter to every person with the same last surname in the town where her birth parents were from. One woman who got such a letter pulled it out of the desk drawer she had stashed it in and spontaneously read it on the local radio station while announcing her yard sale. Amazingly, it resulted in a match! Fate does step in.

Just write that you are looking for a lost family friend and keep it simple. Inserting your birth date will safely let the person you are searching for know who you are and yet protect their privacy at the same time. They will greatly appreciate this. Do not mention birth parents, siblings, adoption, etc., in your letter. If you get a phone call from the addressee instead of the person you are searching for and they ask questions, be polite, but ask them to give your phone number to the right person so you can talk to them directly. Just tell them it is personal, and do not explain. Never tell a third party something this personal, as your birth family member may want this kept private and you could ruin your chances of a good reception.

Sign your letter and make as many copies as there are surnames in the area phone book. Here is one example of what you might want write:

Date

YOUR NAME
Your Street
Your City, State and zip
Your phone number
Your email address if you have one
Dear (insert last name) family member,

I am helping my mother search for a long lost friend of hers and I am wondering if you might be related or know how I can locate (him or her)? (Her or His) name is (insert name here) and she last saw (her or him) in your area on (your birth date). (Optional last sentence if a woman) She may have married and have a different last name now.

If you know (their name)'s whereabouts, could you please pass this letter on to (him or her) or give (him or her) my contact information along with the information in the above paragraph?

If you can help, thank you so much for your time.

Sincerely,

Your written signature

Your typed name

Social Security

Try to get a copy of your original social security card. Tell them you lost yours. Often women who are pregnant will be on welfare and the State will have the baby assigned a social security number right away. This will list your birth parents names as well as your original given name at birth.

You can verify up to five names or Social Security Numbers by calling the toll free number for the Social Security Administration at 800-772-1213. They are open for service weekdays from 7:00 a.m. to 7:00 p.m. in all times zones.

The Social Security Death Index is a resource that may or may not bring results but is worth a try. This is a free website to search. www.familytreelegends.com/records/ssdi

State Birth Indexes

For a small fee, many states will allow you to search their birth index if they have one. This is time consuming, but has been proven to produce results for the names of birth parents. A common thing to look for is a baby with no first name as many birth mother's did not officially give their child a name. If you do not live in the state where these files are located, find a search angel who can do this for you. If a search angel is not listed from the state you need, they may know someone who is.

Another great search website with a multitude of resources too numerous to list and categorize is at: http://stevemorse.org/ It's surprisingly well worth the visit.

Prior to 1970 the Health Departments in some states would publish books yearly with birth records listed for every county. These records contained the names of children who were being put up for adoption along with the maiden name of the birth mother. Many of these books were destroyed but a few small county archives still have them.

Universities & Colleges

If you have located the names of your birth parents and know where they went to college you can write to the registrar of the school and request records. Here is an example of a letter you might write to the registrar to obtain more information.

Date

University or College Name
Registrar of Student Records
Street Address
City, State and Zip

Dear Registrar *(or their name if you can get it)*:

I would like to request information on a former student of yours named *(name)* who would have attended *(name of college or university)* around *(year)*? I understand that some data is not confidential and can be released. In that light, will you please send me as much of the following information as is available?

Dates of attendance, major field of study, address when applied, next of kin, degrees earned, last school attended, age at application, organizations belonged to, and full name at time of application.

Enclosed is a self-addressed-stamped envelope for your convenience. *(Don't forget to include this!)* I look forward to hearing back from you soon. Thank you.

Respectfully,

Your written signature

Your Typed Name
Your Street
Your City, State and zip
Your phone number
Your email address if you have one

Court House Records

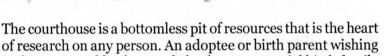

The courthouse is a bottomless pit of resources that is the heart of research on any person. An adoptee or birth parent wishing to do a personal background check on a potential birth family member can find more information than they may realize.

Most courthouse records are available to the public and are full of information on just about anyone in the county who has had any dealings with the court for any number of reasons. The County Clerk as well as other departments would have car and mobile home registrations, business licenses, property records, traffic tickets, tax records, circuit and civil court records, voters registration, fishing and hunting licenses, small claims court records, marriage and divorce records, building permits, probate records, and depending on your state's laws, police and/or criminal records. Here are a few examples of helpful information found in a courthouse:

- If a business relies on drivers for deliveries, etc. a courthouse check on driver's license records for reckless driving or DWI arrests would be invaluable for extra information.
- The general indexing at the courthouse could also produce valuable information, especially if lawsuits have been filed against them in either civil or circuit court.
- Social Security numbers can show up on any number of courthouse records for identification purposes.

Whether the courthouse uses old ledger systems, microfiche or computer systems or a combination thereof, the information is there to find. Sometimes court clerks will help you look up the indexes, which are usually sectioned by the year or month and then alphabetized by name.

Not all of this information can be found in one department at the courthouse so the researcher will need to make the rounds to the different records departments to gather all the available information. There are always research companies and independent contractors available for a fee if you can't find a search angel in the state you need and don't have the resources to do the research yourself. Furthermore, some departments may not be willing to let you have access to these records. In this instance, it would be beneficial to hire a research professional who does have access to the information you need.

No department has the right to seal a public record at the request of a citizen. The public cannot decide what information is to be public. Contact your local county attorney if your request is denied because the information you request is a matter of public record.

Copies can be expensive; so take pencils and a notebook in order to write down every single detail found on the records. Also check all possible resources. There can be more than one marriage, either in a woman's maiden name or her previous married name, so don't quit with just one marriage record.

Check city tax records, assumed name certificates - aka fictitious name, and business licenses.

Request Copies of Veterans Military Personnel Records at: www.archives.gov. Military deaths are indexed and can be searched on several online websites. These include causalities from most wars going back to WWI.

The following link will take you to a free automated open records law letter generator that helps people obtain access to public records maintained by state or local government officials. www.splc.org/ltr_sample.html

To check property owners go to the state website and find the link to the County Assessor's office.

Public Records in Depth
by Joseph J. Culligan

Do you have a name but nothing else? The county is the depository of many records that can be searched by hand. There are hundreds of different records that may assist you in finding the person you are looking for.

Alarm Registrations

There is an investigative technique that I frequently use that surprises everyone. It is called the "alarm registration."

When someone uses an alarm/security company (for example Brinks) that person must complete a registration form for that company. That person also has to fill out an application to the local government. The application filled out for Brinks is not public information, but the one made out to the local government is.

The reason you fill out an application for the local government is so that the government will have a way to contact you if your alarm goes off more than three times in a year. If this does occur, you will be given a fine (that is the rule of thumb for most governments). The application you fill out is a public document because there is a relationship between you and the government. Since they can fine or tax you, that record must be open to public inspection.

I have always used public records to the greatest extent possible because of the consistency that they provide my investigations. To depend heavily on a data base provider who supplies records out of the mainstream has many pitfalls and not just legal ones. Since they are simply not dependable, you do not want to have your entire search hinging on information from a broker.

An alarm registration of an individual or company can be looked up by name or address. The record is usually found at the communications department that handles 911 calls for the jurisdiction or municipality that you are searching. For instance, in Dade County, Florida, it would be the Dade County Police and Fire Communications Bureau, but in Miami where they have their own 911 system, it would be with them.

The typical application will contain your name and telephone number. If it is unlisted, it still has to be listed on the application because they need to contact you. No one gives a wrong telephone number to the police department on an application like this, so you can be assured that the telephone number is good. This is a great way to get unlisted telephone numbers.

The next information listed on the application is place of employment and its telephone number. This is a good way to find out where someone works.

The next bit of information listed — the next of kin or someone who is allowed to go into the house or give authorization to the police to go into the house — is what is most important to me when finding someone who is difficult to locate. The person who is listed is someone, as you can imagine, who is very close to the subject. No other document that is so readily available gives you a person that may know where your subject is.

There are two distinct files I ask for. First, I ask for a copy of the original application because the current information may list an employer from years ago who is not on the present printout. Also, a next of kin may be listed on the original application who is not currently listed on the computer screen. Remember this is important because the person listed on an application from many years ago and who is not listed now may have an ax to grind against your missing person and could possibly give you a lot of valuable information.

When you pass by the residence of your subject, you can see if they have a sign that says Brinks or some other alarm company. Although, I do not make the observation of a sign the criteria as to whether or not someone has an alarm. I simply get a list of all the addresses where my subject has lived at and run those addresses. Old addresses are fine to run because you still want old applications since they can provide just as much information (such as former employers and next of kin).

You can usually contact the local police and fire departments to retrieve a copy of the orginal application and, most importantly, a printout of what is shown on the computer screen (which would give you the most current information).

In a major political case a few years ago, I was able to get the unlisted numbers of several people. I had to revisit the story again later, and when I requested the information I was refused. I called the Commander of the Communications Department who knew who I was. He said that he had new applications printed that had a box that can be checked off by an applicant to indicate whether he or she would allow information to be released if requested by a third party. I told the commander he could not do that. He said he could.

I contacted the county attorney and said that no department had the right unilaterally and arbitrarily to make a public record not public at the request of a citizen. I explained that the tax collector could have the same box on tax forms so people could keep their property tax records confidential. Or a person could check a box on the divorce records and keep them secret. The county attorney understood. Once again I stress: the public cannot decide what information is to be public!

The commander was told by the county attorney that he had no authority to close up public records at the request of a party and that he was to immediately open the alarm registration records to public inspection for me and anyone else.

Pet Licenses

Pet licenses are records that I always ask for in an investigation. If the subject owns a pet, I am sure I will be able to find him or her because I know that anyone who owns an animal who is dear to them will have the pet registered.

Check the counties in the state you think your subject may be in. Dog licenses are a matter of public record, and they are listed by the owners' name. Every person who cares as much about their dog as most people do will not only keep their dog licensed, but they will also give correct information, such as home address and telephone number so that they can be contacted in the event the dog is missing. No one gives false information on a pet license if they ever want the animal reunited with them in the event of his disappearance.

Military Records

Throughout life people have many difficulties, and some may be inclined to change parts of their background to conceal things from others. I always order military records since they inevitably prove to be a good source of "real" information on a subject. A person generates military records at a younger age than most other records, and military records are frozen in time so you can be assured that they have not been changed or deleted in any way. Here are some of the ways I use military records.

Part of the records you receive from the military will contain Past Duty Assignments. These are very important. If your subject had been stationed in San Diego, you will be able to search the public records for criminal or civil actions in that area. Perhaps there was a paternity suit or a marriage. Or perhaps a divorce after the marriage. Also past military assignments will give me a clear picture if the subject has been trained in explosives or is an expert in artillery, including guns. I need to tell the client that the subject has a background that has a generous sprinkling of skills that she or he may need to know so that they can protect themselves or even obtain a restraining order. Remember restraining orders are not just for battered wives.

Also, do not overlook the awards and decorations that the subject received. These will give you a clearer picture of where the subject was when he was in the service. Some special decorations are for special forces, such as the Army Rangers or Navy Seals. Also, many intelligence officers are recruited from the military.

Editors Note: An application form to request military records can be found at: www.goodmanlaw.com/pdf/mil-rcrds.pdf

This article on Public Records was taken from the book *Business Security: Over 50 Ways to Protect Your Small Business.*

Modified excerpt from Joseph Culligan's book, *You Can Find Anybody.*

Voter's Registration

Voter's registration information is available upon written request. Write to the county you believe your subject may have been or is registered in.

It is easy to ascertain a subject's date of birth and home address. In one case, the only information I had was that at one time the subject named Lub lived in Baldwin, New York. Since I was not supplied a first name, I wrote to the Board of Elections of the county of jurisdiction for Baldwin. I sent a nominal fee of $3.00 since this is the average cost of requesting voter's registration records.

I requested that I be sent the voter's registration information of every person named Lub in Baldwin. In this case I was fortunate that my request was for an unusual name. I learned that the subject, Lub, did not live in Baldwin any longer and had moved in 1985. The subject's new address was 140 Larch Street, Wantagh, New York. The response I received also included the subject's date of birth. Since I was aware that my subject had been in a serious accident on a certain date and at a certain location, I asked for the subject's driving record.

To be able to write one letter and be provided with a full name for the subject makes this one of the best searching techniques.

Joseph Culligan is a licensed private investigator and the author of *You Can Find Anybody!*, *When In Doubt, Check Him Out,* and *Manhunt: The Book.* He is a Hall of Fame member of the National Association of Investigative Specialists. Mr. Culligan has been featured on shows such as Montel, Maury Povich, CNN, Hard Copy, Unsolved Mysteries, and many more. To contact Mr. Culligan or to purchase his books go to his website at: www.JosephCulligan.com.

Find a Reputable P.I.

When you've exhausted all the legal requirements your state demands from you and the courts still deny you your birth information, hiring an investigator may be another option for you. If you can afford to hire someone to help you in your search you want to make sure that you find someone who is reliable and has experience in birth family searches. You may never have used an investigator before and know little, if anything, about what it entails outside of the romantic side seen on television. With that in mind, how does the average person know how to find an ethical and reputable PI who will do a good job? This detailed article was written after an extensive survey from nearly 2,000 PIs who have set their own high standards for their industry.

A very high percentage of licensed PI's are former or retired Law Enforcement Officers, FBI, Secret Service, or Military personnel, and with the exception of the few states listed below that don't require licensing, have to go through extensive training in order to qualify for licensing in their state. Looking in the yellow pages for a private investigator is akin to being a kid again and saying eenie, meenie, minee, moe. Additionally, bigger ads do not mean better PI's. Many good PI's maintain a low-profile image.

These are the states that do not require licensing for a private investigator at this time — Alabama, Alaska, Colorado, Idaho, Kentucky, Mississippi, Missouri, South Dakota, and Wyoming. In-house company investigators who do not work outside of the company may not be subject to licensing laws in the remaining states. Check with your state for in-house investigator requirements if you are considering implementing such a department within your company.

Here are the most important opinions of nearly 2,000 PI's who were polled on how they would go about finding a reputable private investigator. As you can see, these professionals hold themselves up to the highest of standards:

- Ask your local highest-ranking law enforcement officials. They have very likely run into PI's, both good and bad, in the course of their job. They may be able to offer opinions on who they deem as having quality and ethics, as well as who to stay away from.
- Ask an attorney, paralegal, or even a law office's legal secretary – the secretary may know a lot more than what her boss might.
- If you know of other people who have frequently used PI's, ask for their opinion. Word of mouth is often the best advertising for a good investigator.
- Interview the PI's you are considering. Ask these types of questions: How long have they been licensed? What type of cases do they specialize in? How much training have they had in the type of case you need them for (don't hire a traffic accident expert for a criminal defense case)? If they do not work your type of case, will they recommend someone who does? Are they qualified to testify in court in cases like yours if necessary? If you are working with an attorney, have they worked with your attorney or the opposing attorney before?
- See if they appear professional in their dress and manner, not slovenly and disorganized.
- Make sure you feel comfortable and compatible with the PI you select.
- Always ask their fees up front and have them list what expenses they require you to pay for and how often they require those payments. If they are evasive in telling you, remember "caveat emptor." An honest PI will tell you right up front what their fees are and what their time is worth. Cheap is not necessarily good and expensive is not necessarily better. One PI explained the charges for their services very well when he said, "People will pay a plumber $75 an hour to change a water heater, but complain about paying an investigator $100 an hour to risk his life hunting down witnesses or bad guys."
- Ask for references and then follow through by checking them.

- Never hire a PI who guarantees results, but rather one who offers a contract that states what they will do for their fees. There should also be a statement in the contract stating that you will receive detailed reports for the time spent. You want to see what you are paying for!

- A description of the case should also be included in the contract, and you and your investigator need to discuss ahead of time how to approach your case. If there are special circumstances that will dictate this approach, you will need to make your investigator aware of it. Observe if the investigator is seriously listening to your advice in handling a sensitive issue.

- Please remember that the investigator you are hiring is not in the handholding business, and he will have many other cases he is working on besides your own. The time you spend on the phone with him is costing you money and him time, much the same as talking to an attorney. A busy and reputable investigator will definitely charge you for all phone calls after the initial free consultation. This is a business expense and will come out of your retainer. On the other hand, there may be times when it is imperative that you be able to reach your investigator. Will he/she provide 24/7 accesses?

- Find out if the PI is a member of the local Chamber of Commerce and what other organizations he or she belongs to. Check the Better Business Bureau to see if there have been any complaints filed against him or her, or anyone else within their agency.

- Check the courthouse records to see if disgruntled clients have sued the PI or anybody he or she works with.

- Contact the State PI Association in the state where they work. The Secretary of State will be able to give you that contact information or you can find it listed on the Internet at: www.pimall.com/nais/pi.assoc.list.html. The State Licensing agency will also be able to tell you if any complaints have been filed against the PI's agency or the individual PI in question.

- Find a PI who is computer savvy and has an email address and fax machine. Computers play a very important role in today's investigations. Although legwork is still a necessary part of investigations, the days of Sam Spade are no longer enough.
- Make sure that the PI is fully covered with verifiable Errors & Omissions insurance to avoid any possibility of your getting in the middle of a lawsuit if your investigator makes a serious sueable mistake.
- Be wary if an investigator assures you that he can guarantee the outcome of the case. Things often are not as simple as they seem and can change at a moment's notice. A wise investigator knows that.
- Make sure that the contract has a confidentiality clause and that the party being investigated will not be informed of the investigation. The exception to this would be a signed release of information form from an employee or possible new employee being considered for a job. Most PI's will readily guarantee confidentiality. However, be aware that the confidentiality between yourself and the investigator can only be guaranteed as far as the law allows. A PI can be subpoenaed to testify in a court of law. Check your state laws or ask your attorney. It is your responsibility to find out the law, know it well, and be prepared.

There are also a few professional organizations that can help you find qualified of investigators anywhere in the world:

The NCISS is an organization in which all PI's are eligible to join. The NCISS is also their lobbying venue.

National Council of Investigation & Security Services
NCISS Headquarters Washington D.C.
1730 M Street, N.W., Suite 200
Washington, D.C. 20036
www.nciss.com/

The National Association of Investigative Specialists (NAIS) is the world's largest association of professional private investigators with over 3,500 members from around the world. You can search for professionals by state, city, or country and you can review their various investigative areas of expertise at: www.pinais.com

The following two organizations are by invitation only, and each PI is thoroughly checked out before he is considered for membership. These would be excellent sources for highly qualified private investigators.

W.A.D
World Association of Detectives
Brough, HU15 1XL, England
Ph: +44-1482-665577
Fax: +44 870-831-0957
wad@wad.net www.wad.net/

INTELNET
International Intelligence Network
P.O. Box 350
Gladwyne, PA 19035
Ph: 610-687-2999 or 800-784-2020
Fax: 800-784-2020
intelnet@bellatlantic.net
www.intelnetwork.org/about.asp

Waiver of Confidentiality

The following form template is formatted to fit an adoptee, but birth parents can copy and modify it to fit their needs as well. All words in italics without parenthesis are to be changed to your own personal information. Information in parenthesis is for directions only. Do not type your information in italics in your document. Please take further note that for legal forms the font Courier New as shown in the letter below is suggested, size 10, 11, or even 12 on standard sized white paper of 8.5" x 11" and with justified margins. The following Waiver of Confidentiality as well as the following forms have been minimized to fit this book size.

The original notarized Waiver of Confidentiality should be placed with your original birth certificate at the Department of Health, then send copies to the state registrar, adoption agency, and the attorney who handled your adoption (if there was one). Also include a copy of your current birth certificate and driver's license or other legal identification. All of this should be done before you attempt to Petition the Court. However, in several states this Waiver is all you need for access to your records.

A state-by-state listing of the Departments of Health is included at the back of this book.

After you finish typing your Waiver, do NOT sign it until you are in front of a Notary Public (usually a free service at your bank). After notarization, make copies for the other agencies and an extra copy for your *own* records. Mail the Waivers with a return-receipt request so you will have records showing the date and name of the person who received it. Be sure to mail the *original* Waiver that you signed in front of a Notary to the Department of Health.

Always submit a self-addressed-stamped envelope with your Waiver for them to send you your information in. You may also include a sealed envelope with a letter, pictures, etc. to be placed in your file and given to your birth family should they request information of you. You may also request in your Waiver your appreciation if they would forward the sealed letter to your birth family.

If by chance you were born in one state and your adoption was finalized in another, submit your Waiver in *both* states. Make sure all your bases are covered.

IMPORTANT: You are *not* required to sign a release form for this information. If they refuse your request without the release form, you can tell them that you will report them to the state licensing board and then follow through if they do not comply.

WAIVER OF CONFIDENTIALITY

YOUR NAME
Your Street
Your City, State and zip
Your area code and phone number

Office of Vital Records *(locations found in back of book)*
The Department of Health
Address
Your City, State and zip

To All Concerned Parties:

I hereby formally request that this letter and/or copies of it immediately be placed in all records and files you have pertaining to my adoption as handled through The Department of Health and finalized *date*, in *name of* Court. My adopted name is *your name* and I was born on *your birth date* at *name of* Hospital in *City, State and zip*. Copies of my current birth certificate and driver's license or other legal identification are included with this authorization letter.

Please consider this letter and/or copies of it to be my legal authorization to waive the confidentiality due me by any law(s) and/or organizations of *birth State* regarding anything considered to be identifying information.

I want the effects of this letter to extend only to my birth mother, birth father, and any birth siblings I may have. It is my desire that the following information be released in full: my full name, current address and telephone number as found above, and all records in my files, including any updated information I may give you in the future.

By this waiver, I give you full and legal permission to release my present identity and whereabouts as given above. This waiver shall remain in full effect until revoked by myself in writing. I have enclosed a self-addressed-stamped-envelope for your convenience and I look forward to your quick response.

DATED this _____ day of _____ 20____ .

Respectfully Submitted By:

_____

Your Name typed here

SUBSCRIBED and SWORN to before me on
this _____ day of _____, 20___ .

_____
NOTARY PUBLIC

Non-Id Request

This letter is handled the same way as the Waiver of Confidentiality; so the following directions are a repeat in case you didn't read the Waiver section.

The following form template is formatted to fit an adoptee but birth parents can copy and modify it to fit their needs as well. All words in italics without parenthesis should be changed to your own personal information. Information in parenthesis is for directions only. Do not type your information in italics in your document.

As with the Waiver, for legal forms the font Courier New is suggested, size 10 or 11 on standard sized white paper of 8.5" x 11" and with justified margins. The following Non-Id Request has been minimized to fit this page size. Also, do not forget to send the self-addressed-stamped envelope with your request if you want the information sent to you.

Send this completed letter to the Department of Health with copies going to the Adoption Agency, State Registrar, and/or Attorney that handled your adoption if there was one. You should also include a copy of your current birth certificate and driver's license. Be sure to include a self-addressed stamped envelope for their reply. The letter with your original notarized signature on it gets mailed to the Department of Health, with the copies going to the other agencies. A state-by-state listing of the Departments of Health is included at the back of this book.

 After you finish typing your Non-Id Request, do NOT sign it until you are in front of a Notary Public (usually a free service at your bank). After it's notarized, make copies for the other agencies and an extra copy for your *own* records. Mail the Waivers with return-receipt requests so you will have records showing the date and name of the person who received it. Be sure to mail the ORIGINAL Waiver that you signed in front of a Notary to the Department of Health.

You are NOT required to sign a release form for this information. If they refuse your request without the release form, you can tell them that you will report them to the state licensing board.

Non-Identifying information can give you great clues to help further your search. It may tell you the date and place of the adoptee's birth, ages of both birth parents, number of other children, ethnicity, race, hair and eye colors and education levels and occupations at the time of the birth as well as the reason for placing the child for adoption. Medical history may also be included.

It should give you enough information so that you can contact the State Archives and request information for the birth indexes in the town or county of your birth. If the birth index is not kept in State Archives, try to locate where it is being stored. The county librarian should be able to direct you.

If by chance you were born in one state and your adoption was finalized in another, apply for your non-id information in *both* states. You may get extra information from one that is not on the other.

Once again, whenever you are dealing with government officials or birth family relatives, do not use the word adoption or the door may be slammed in your face. Genealogical research or looking for lost family members are the most common reasons to be asking for records.

NON-ID REQUEST

YOUR NAME
Your Street
Your City, State and zip
Your area code and phone number

Office of Vital Records *(locations found in back of book)*
The Department of Health
Address
Your City, State and zip

Re: Request for Identifying or Non-Identifying Information

To Whom It May Concern:

I am a mature adult adoptee and I hereby formally request
photocopies of the original following records that are held
in my file as opposed to a summary:

> Identifying Information
> Non-Identifying Information
> Petition To Adopt
> Relinquishment papers
> Change of Name
> Certificate of Adoption
> Adoption Decree
> Finalized Court Papers

My adopted name is *Your Name* and I was born on *your birth date*
at *Your birth* Hospital in *City, State and zip*. My adoption was
finalized on *your adoption date* [**OR** I do not know the date that
my adoption was finalized].

The names of my adoptive parents are:

> *adoptive mother*
> *adoptive father*

In the alternative, I would greatly appreciate answers to as
many of the questions below as possible.

What name was I given at birth?
What was the name of the hospital I was born in?
What was the name of the attending physician?
Do I have brothers or sisters?
What are their names and ages?
What are the nationalities of my birth parents?
Were my birth parents married, and if so, for how long
    before the adoption?
What were the occupations of my birth parents?
How old were my birth parents at the time of my adoption?
What was the physical description of my birth parents?
What are my birth parents names?

When and where were my birth parents born?
What were the religious preferences of my birth parents?
Was I baptized? If so, where?
What was the education level of my birth parents?
Were my birth parents members of any branch of the military
or reserves?
Was I ever in foster care as an infant? Group home?
         Maternity home?
Which court finalized this adoption?
What was the judge's name?
Did both my birth mother and birth father sign
         relinquishment papers?
Who did the home study on the adoptive parents?
Was medical information on my birth parents left in my
         file?

If you are unable to comply with my request, please cite the
specific law that prohibits the release of this information to
me and please advise me where I should write to obtain the
information. I have enclosed a self-addressed-stamped-envelope
for your convenience and I look forward to your quick response.

Copies of my current birth certificate and driver's license or
other legal identification are included with this legal
authorization letter.

DATED this _____ day of _____ 20_____ .

                    Respectfully Submitted By:

          _____

                    Your Name typed here

SUBSCRIBED and SWORN to before me on
this _____ day of _____ , 20___ .

_____

NOTARY PUBLIC

Copied to: *(list names of adoption agency and/or attorney. If
not known, delete this part)*

Court Headings

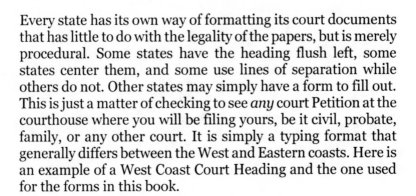

Every state has its own way of formatting its court documents that has little to do with the legality of the papers, but is merely procedural. Some states have the heading flush left, some states center them, and some use lines of separation while others do not. Other states may simply have a form to fill out. This is just a matter of checking to see *any* court Petition at the courthouse where you will be filing yours, be it civil, probate, family, or any other court. It is simply a typing format that generally differs between the West and Eastern coasts. Here is an example of a West Coast Court Heading and the one used for the forms in this book.

```
[name]
[address]
[city], [state] [zip]
[phone]
Petitioner Pro Se



        IN THE [DISTRICT, FAMILY, ETC.] COURT OF THE

    STATE OF [STATE] IN AND FOR THE COUNTY OF [COUNTY]
_____
                                )
[YOUR NAME],                    ) CASE NO.:
                                ) Adoption File No.:
                                ) Department:
          Petitioner.           )
_____  )
```

Here is sample heading from a specific Court in Florida. They do not list a name and address at the top of the page and as you can see, they use no lines for dividing sections. The following heading is another example of one found on the internet. All three headings are vastly different.

IN THE CIRCUIT COURT OF THE EIGHTH JUDICIAL CIRCUIT,

IN AND FOR ALACHUA COUNTY, FLORIDA

Case No: 0000-0

Division: _____

IN RE: THE ADOPTION OF

John Doe

Adoptee(s).

IN THE COURT OF COMMON PLEAS OF WESTMORELAND COUNTY,
PENNSYLVANIA ORPHANS'COURT DIVISION

IN RE: ADOPTION OF   )
)
        JOHN DOE   ) No.: _____ of (date)
        (post-adoption name))
)
)
) PETITION TO APPOINT
) BIRTHPARENT SEARCH AGENT
) ON BEHALF OF AN ADULT
) ADOPTEE
)
)
) Filed on behalf of:
) JOHN DOE
)
) Counsel of Record
) ATTORNEY NAME, Esquire
)
) Supreme Court I.D. No.
)
) 156 Clay Pike
) North Huntingdon, PA 15642
)
) (724) 861-8333

Affidavit

Basic directions in Waiver of Confidentiality and Non-Id Request apply here as well. Please read them first.

In some states an Affidavit may be all that is required to access your sealed information. If that is the case for your state, this Affidavit should be enough. This document should be filed in the state and the county where you were born and where your original birth certificate is located. It also needs to be filed in the proper court that handles adoption record requests. An online website to find all country courthouse locations can be found at: www.genealogy.com/00000229.html

Once you have printed out your finished documents, you can use them as templates for any changes you may need in order to conform to your state's requirements (or file them at your court if they conform). The court clerk should tell you if they are okay for filing. These are the steps you need to take for this document.

1. Before typing up the document, make a "check list" with all the information you are going to need. This will give you the time to obtain all the necessary dates, names, places, and contacts; including copies of your current birth certificate, driver's license, and letter from your doctor (if needed) to use as attachments. Once you have all the items on your "check list," typing out your document will go much faster and easier. Instead of having to constantly stop and search for the answers to requested information, you will already have it right at your fingertips.

2. Find out which court to file your papers in. You will need this for your form as well. The court clerk should be able to tell you where it has to be filed if you do not already know.

3. Obtain your current official birth certificate complete with the raised seal on it. This will have to be attached to the original legal document. Make copies of this birth certificate,

your driver's license, and any medical records and letter from your doctor if you are filing for medical reasons. You will need these "exhibits" to attach to your original Affidavit.

4. Make five one-sided copies of **everything**, which will total six including your original. You may not need that many, but some courts require three copies for themselves. If you wish, you can always call the court clerk and ask how many copies they need. Just remember, they won't answer legal questions about the document itself. The Court always gets the original because they require your original signature and not a photocopied one so don't lose track of your original. A sticky note on it will help due to the clarity of copies these days.

5. Sign your finished Affidavit with attached "exhibits" *in front of a Notary*.

6. Staple each set of your Affidavits, including copies of your current birth certificate and medical records behind the Affidavit legal document, in the upper left hand corner. One complete set will be yours to keep. Make sure you write your case number on top of each and every copy when the court clerk gives it to you (if you do not have one already). You will need this number for anything pertaining to your case from this time forward.

7. You need to sign and date the attached Mailing Certificate at the end of the Affidavit on the day you actually mail the copies out – generally the same day you file your papers; so the original Mailing Certificate will be signed. Mail one copy to the adoption agency and/or attorney and one to the health department that is listed in the Certificate of Mailing on the end page of your Affidavit.

Give two or three copies of the Order to the court clerk *if and when* the Judge grants your Affidavit request. If it is granted, you will need this Order to obtain your records from the Department of Vital Statistics.

There will be filing fees at the courthouse when you file your documents. If you cannot afford the filing fees and you can verify your low income, ask the Court Clerk if they have a form you can fill out to request a waiver of court costs and filing fees. In some states this form is called an "Informa Pauperis" or "Affidavit of Impecuniosity." This form will most likely be an Affidavit declaring your assets and income that you will need to sign in front of a Notary Public.

Just remember, when you type out your own legal documents, they will look different than they do in this book. Your page size will widen, you will have more space than is used here, your lines will not take up as much space and your pages will be shorter. Adjust your headers accordingly. Your signature line always needs at least two lines from the previous paragraph above the date to be on the same page. This format is for *ALL* legal documents.

YOUR NAME
Your Street
Your City, State and zip
Your area code and phone number
Petitioner Pro Se

IN THE (*Your Court*) COURT OF THE

STATE OF *STATE* IN AND FOR THE COUNTY OF *COUNTY*

	)
YOUR NAME,	) CASE NO.
	) Adoption File No._____
	) Department:
Petitioner.	)
	)

AFFIDAVIT FOR ACCESS TO SEALED ADOPTION RECORDS

STATE OF *[your state]*   )
) SS.
COUNTY OF *[your county]*   )

I, *[YOUR NAME]*, being first duly sworn, upon my oath do solemnly swear under penalty of perjury that:

1. I am a resident of *[county]* County. My address is *[street]*, *[city]*, *[state]* *[zip]* and my phone number is *[telephone]*.

2. I am a mature adult adoptee and was born on *[birth date]* at *[birth hospital]* Hospital in *[city]*, *[state]*, *[county]* County and was adopted by *[adoptive father]* and *[adoptive mother]* and they gave me the name of *[adoption name]*.

3. *[Insert paragraph #3 from the choices following this Affidavit that most fits your situation.]*

4. *[Insert paragraph #4 from the choices following this Affidavit that most fits your situation.]*

5. I give full and legal permission to release my present identity and whereabouts as given above to my immediate birth family effective for 99 years, even after my death.

6. I authorize the administrator and the administrator's designees to inspect all vital statistic records, court

64

records, and agency records, including confidential records, relating to my birth, marriage, and divorce (as applicable) to the birth and death of any sibling or adoption of myself.

7. Copies of my current birth certificate and driver's license or other legal identification are attached to this Affidavit.

8. I believe that I have good cause to inspect the contents of my birth records in their entirety.

DATED this _____ day of _____, 20____ .

_____
[your name]

SUBSCRIBED and SWORN to before me
this _____ day of _____, 20___

_____
NOTARY PUBLIC
My Commission Expires: _____

CERTIFICATE OF MAILING

I HEREBY CERTIFY that on the _____ day of _____, 20____, I served a true and correct copy of the foregoing AFFIDAVIT TO UNSEAL ADOPTION RECORDS by depositing a copy of the same in the United States mail via First Class Mail, postage prepaid, addressed as follows:

Bureau of vital statistics name found in this book
address
city, state, zip

[attorney or agency name]
[attorney or agency street]
[attorney or agency city, state and zip)

_____
[type your name here]

*(only include addresses if applicable and do not type **this** italiced line.)*

Affidavit Sentence Choices

3. My adoption was handled by *(name of agency or attorney)*.

3. I do not know the name of the agency or attorney who handled my adoption.

4. I have a medical need for health information of genetic significance that may affect my physical or mental health. A letter from my physician is attached. *[Medical reasons from your doctor are the best choice if you have that option.]*

4. I am contemplating a future with children and believe that I have a responsibility to know about my natural family's medical and genealogical background for my family.

4. I have children and believe that I have a responsibility to know about my natural family's medical and genealogical background for my family.

Order on Affidavit

YOUR NAME
Your Street
Your City, State and zip
Your area code and phone number
Petitioner Pro Se

IN THE *ADOPTION* COURT OF THE

STATE OF *STATE* IN AND FOR THE COUNTY OF *COUNTY*

	)
YOUR NAME,	) CASE NO.
	) Adoption File No._____
	) Department:
Petitioner.	)
	)

ORDER ON AFFIDAVIT FOR ACCESS TO SEALED ADOPTION RECORDS

The Affidavit for access to sealed adoption records of the above-named child having been filed in this Court, and notice having been given to necessary parties, NOW, and upon all the papers and proceedings herein, it is hereby ORDERED that the Affidavit is GRANTED and that *YOUR NAME* shall be given access to sealed identifying adoption records for good cause showing on the grounds that (*Type in here one of the three options listed on the next page only don't type in the number. It needs to be the same option for paragraph #4 that you selected in your Affidavit, but just replaced with the wording from the following page.*)

DATED this _____ day of _____, 20____.

_____
PRESIDING JUDGE

67

Order Sentence Choices

Do not include the number in front of the sentence in your document.

1. *(she or he)* has a medical need for health information of genetic significance that may affect *(his or her)* physical or mental health.

2. *(she or he)* has children and *(she or he)* has a responsibility to know about *(his or her)* natural family's medical and genealogical background for *(his or her)* family.

3. *(she or he)* is contemplating a future with children and has a responsibility to know about *(his or her)* natural family's medical and genealogical background for *(his or her)* family.

Doctor's Letter

Before you go to your doctor's appointment to discuss your need of a letter from him explaining the medical reasons for why you should have your adoption records opened, you might want to type up an example letter in order to give him an idea of what the court needs. The doctor may just surprise you and sign the one you take rather than type up another one. Here is a sample letter:

Date *(of your appointment)*

Doctor's Name
Doctor's Address
Doctor's Phone number

     Re: *(Your Full Name and address)*

To the Court:

(Your Name) has no medical history available because *(he/she)* is adopted. It is my belief that my patient's mental and physical health may be at risk without knowledge of *(his/her)* biological parents and their medical history, biological heritage, religious, genetic, ethnic, and genealogical origin. This ongoing concern could also affect (his/her) children or future children.

The only way to anticipate and prevent what physical or mental conditions of genetic significance that may affect *[his/her]* physical or emotional mental health is to have knowledge of *(his/her)* biological family's complete medical and background history.

Sincerely,

(Type Doctor's name here)

State Statutes

The following Statutes that you will insert in the following Petition where indicated are "for good cause showing" which is required for Petitions in most states. The double overlapping S (§) can be replaced with the word "Section" (without the quotes) if you cannot find the right symbol in your font database (under symbols).

Alabama Code § 22-9A-12(c)-(d)
Alaska Statutes § 25-23-150 (d)(1)
Arizona Revised Statutes Title 8-121 (d)
Arkansas Statutes § 9-9-506 (c)
California Family Law Code § 9203 (a)
Colorado Revised Statutes § 19-5-301
Connecticut General Statutes § 45a-751
Delaware Code, Title 13, § 962
District of Columbia Title 16, Chapter 3 §16-311
Florida Statutes Chapter 63, § 63.162(7)
Georgia Code § 19-8-23
Hawaii Revised Statutes § 578-15
Idaho Statutes Title 16 § 16-1511
Illinois Compiled Statutes 750 ILCS 50 §18.1 et seq.
Indiana Revised Statutes § IC 31-19-21, § IC 31-19-25-2
Iowa Code § 600.16A
Kansas Statutes § 59-2122
Kentucky Revised Statutes Title XVII Chapter 199.572
Louisiana Ch. C. Art. 1189
Maine Revised Statutes Title 22, Ch. 701, § 2706-A
Maryland Statutes Family Law § 5-359
Massachusetts Chapter 210, § 5D
Michigan Compiled Law § 710.68
Minnesota Statutes § 259.89
Mississippi Code § 93-17-221
Missouri Revised Statutes Chapter 453, § 453.121
Montana Code Annotated Title 42 Ch. 6 § 42-6-103
Nebraska Revised Statutes § 43-113(1)
Nevada Revised Statutes § NRS 127.140
New Hampshire Revised Statutes § 170-B:24

New Jersey Revised Statutes § 9:3-52
New Mexico Statutes § 32A-5-40(F)
New York State Consolidated Laws, DR Ch. 14, Art. 7, Title 2, § 114
North Carolina General Statutes § 48-9-105
North Dakota Century Code § 14-15-16(24)
Ohio Revised Code § 3107.41
Oklahoma Statutes Annotated § 10-7505-1.1(C)
Oregon Revised Statutes § 109.440
Pennsylvania Consolidated Statutes Title 23 Ch. 29 § 2905
Rhode Island General Law § 15-7.2-4
South Carolina Code of Law § 20-7-1780
South Dakota Codified Law § 25-6-15
Tennessee Code § 36-1-138
Texas Family Code § 162.022
Utah Code Annotated § 78-30-15(1)
Vermont Statutes Title 15A, § 6-112
Virginia Code § 63.2-1247(C)
Washington Code Revised, RCW § 26.33.330(1)
West Virginia Code § 48-22-702(b)
Wisconsin Statutes § 48.433(9)
Wyoming § 1-22-203

Petition Introduction

Generally, a person must demonstrate "good cause showing" to a judge why he or she should be granted access to confidential information found within an unaltered adoption file.

These template forms will help you prepare a "Petition To Unseal Adoption Records" with accompanying "Notice," "Affidavit," and "Order" to file with the court where your adoption was finalized. It should not be used until *after* you have first attempted to obtain your information with a Waiver of Confidentiality and a Letter Requesting Non-Identifying Information. Many states have laws already set into place that will provide you with this information without your needing a Petition, and may not recognize a Petition filed prior to the other documents. If you have not submitted these other forms, please go back to the Waiver of Confidentiality and Non-Identifying Information Request. This Petition is the *last* document you should use.

There will be filing fees at the courthouse when you file your documents. If you cannot afford the filing fees and you can verify your low income, ask the Court Clerk if they have a form you can fill out to request a waiver of court costs and filing fees. In some states this form is called an "Informa Pauperis" or "Affidavit of Impecuniosity." This form will most likely be an Affidavit declaring your assets and income that you will need to sign in front of a Notary Public.

If the Judge grants your Petition, the Court may also require nominal fees from you for the search and production of documents, etc.

The statutes used in this Petition are up-to-date to the best of our knowledge and we are not responsible should the laws in your state change or for any mistakes inadvertently made on our part. Please contact Crary Publications if your state is changing its adoption records law or if ours do not conform to your state's requirements. If you want to find the complete state procedures required specifically for your state, you will find the statutes listed online at: www.family.findlaw.com /adoption/state-adoption-laws

Laws are constantly changing and it is your responsibility to be aware of any law changes in the state where you are planning to file your Petition.

When you finish typing your Petition you must also include copies of your current birth certificate, driver's license, and letter from your doctor (if needed) to use as attachments.

If this seems overwhelming, just remember it is a court document that may get you the birth information you need. Take it one-step at a time. It is a slow process and you will need lots of patience. If this is more than you think you can do yourself, please consult an attorney.

One last caveat: You may run into a judge that absolutely does not like Pro Se petitioners. The laws almost always provide for Pro Se petitioners, so you can either further alienate a negative judge by arguing with him, or take what he dishes out when he demands you get an attorney. Then on the other hand, there are countless sympathetic judges who will understand your dilemma and grant your Petition. It's just the luck of the draw.

At the end of these documents, you will find an example of what your completed Petition papers should look like after you have finished typing them with your own information included.

Notice

Please read these instructions carefully. This is a legal court document. These instructions will help you to prepare and file your Petition step-by-step as a "Pro Se" document which means "doing it yourself." That includes typing them yourself with your own information replacing the italicized portions in these forms. If these instructions become too difficult for you, please consult an attorney. Taken one-step at a time, most people should be able to do this. The following are the steps that you will need to take to complete your documents. The first step is the Notice, a small but very important part of the process. The note on the bottom of the Notice is part of the document. Always double-space your documents where shown. Please do NOT rush through this process.

NOTICE: Most states require that you give 30 days notice to the appropriate child placing agency and vital records office prior to your hearing date. File your Notice at the same time as you file your Petition and Affidavit. They will time stamp your documents and give you the date, time, and place for your hearing, which should safely be at least 30 days or more after you file. Put the information they give you on each copy of the Notice, including the one you keep for your personal files. The Notice, Petition, and Affidavit (all filings are time stamped) should be sent by registered or certified mail if you want confirmation of the delivery date (this represents "service"). These papers should be mailed the same day you file them with the court, so give yourself enough time to do both.

When you file your papers, the Court Clerk will assign you a case number (if you don't already have one from your original court adoption case number). Make sure to write that case number down in the space provided for in the court heading on all copies of the Notice, Petition, and Affidavit as everything relating to your case will refer to that number. Do not lose this number! Write it down in your notes even after it is written on your documents.

Name
Address
City, state, zip
Phone
Petitioner Pro Se

IN THE *District, Family, etc.* COURT OF THE

STATE OF *State* IN AND FOR THE COUNTY OF *County*

YOUR NAME,	)	CASE NO.:
	)	Adoption File No.:
	)	Department:
Petitioner.	)	
	)	

NOTICE OF VERIFIED PETITION TO UNSEAL ADOPTION RECORDS

YOU AND EACH OF YOU WILL PLEASE TAKE NOTICE that the undersigned will bring the Verified Petition To Unseal Adoption Records filed on _____, 20___, before the above-entitled Court on the _____day of _____, 20___, at the hour of _____ ___.m. of said day, in Department _____ of said Court.

DATED this _____ day of _____, 20____.

By:_____
Name
Address
City, state, zip
Phone
Petitioner Pro Se

[Note: This Notice of Petition for Access to Sealed Adoption Records is served upon you as required by law. You are not required to appear or to respond. However, should you fail to appear or respond on or before the date set forth in Paragraph 1, it will be assumed you do not object to the relief requested. You may have an attorney appear for you.]

Petition

PETITION & **AFFIDAVIT**: Obtain a new copy of your amended birth certificate from the Department of Vital Statistics with a raised seal on it, attach it at the end of your Petition, and write "EXHIBIT A" on the bottom. Proof of your current address needs to be marked "EXHIBIT B". You could use a copy of your driver's license or legal I.D. or a utility or phone bill with your name and address on it, etc. If you are filing for medical reasons, place the *original* letter from your doctor behind your authentic raised seal amended birth certificate and write "EXHIBIT C" on the bottom.

Before filing your finished Notice, Petition, and Accompanying Affidavit (that you have signed and dated in front of a Notary Public) call the court clerk and ask how many copies they require for their records. Make enough copies of everything the Court requires as well as at least three (3) extra; one for you, one to mail to the adoption agency and/or attorney and one to the health department that you will list in the Certificate of Mailing at the end of your Petition.

Sign and date the **CERTIFICATE OF MAILING** on all copies on the same day you file your papers with the Court, as you will be mailing everything the same day. Staple the Petition, Exhibits, and Mailing Certificate together in the upper left hand corner, and then staple the Affidavit pages together as a separate document.

You should end up with three (3) finished documents in total: the Notice, the Petition, and the Affidavit. The original notarized documents are always filed with the Court because they require your original signature and not a photocopied one to accompany the extra copies they need.

There will be filing fees at the courthouse when you file your documents. If you cannot afford the filing fees and you can verify your low income, ask the Court Clerk if they have a form you can fill out to request a waiver of court costs and filing fees. As stated previously, in some states this Affidavit form is called an "In Forma Pauperis" or "Affidavit of Impecuniosity" that you will need to fill out and sign in front of a Notary Public. This Affidavit declares your assets and income.

The statutes used in this Petition are up-to-date to the best of our knowledge and we are not responsible should the laws in your state change or for any mistakes inadvertently made on our part. Please mail us if your state changes its open adoption records law or if our statutes to do not conform to your states requirements. We update statutes on a yearly basis. If you want to find the complete state procedures required specifically for your state, you will find the statutes listed online at: family.findlaw.com/adoption/state-adoption-laws.

If this seems overwhelming, just remember that this is a court document that may get you the birth information you need. Just take it one-step at a time. It is a slow process and you will need lots of patience. Get help if you need it and are unsure what something means.

These forms are meant only as a guideline for common and standard situations. Each person's situation is unique in nature. If you feel that your particular needs require more specificity than provided with this standard form, you should consult an attorney in your area or go to your local law library and research what you need to know.

Always double-space your documents where shown. At the completion of these document forms for the Petition you will find an example of what your total finished documents will look like when you have typed up your Petition with your own information included.

Name
Address
City, state, zip
Phone
Petitioner Pro Se

IN THE *District, Family, etc.* COURT OF THE

STATE OF *State* IN AND FOR THE COUNTY OF *County*

YOUR NAME,	)	CASE NO.:
	)	Adoption File No.:
	)	Department:
Petitioner.	)	

VERIFIED PETITION FOR ACCESS TO SEALED ADOPTION RECORDS

COMES NOW *[YOUR NAME]*, Petitioner Pro Se, and respectfully petitions the Court to authorize the Clerk of the Court to allow the Petitioner access to all *[his/her]* adoption and birth-record identifying information pursuant to *[insert the statute listed for your state found on page 61]* for good cause showing as follows:

1. That Petitioner *[your name]* is the adoptee in this case and is now a mature adult who was born *[your birth date]* in *[birth city], [birth state]* and was adopted by *[adopted father's name]* and *[adopted mother's name]*. A copy of Petitioner's birth certificate is attached as Exhibit A and proof of current address and legal identification as Exhibit B.

2. *[Insert paragraph #2 from the choices in the section at the end of this petition that most fits your situation.]*

3. That the adoptee has a strong and healthy desire and curiosity to have access to records concerning the identity of *[his/her]* biological parents, biological heritage, religious, genetic, ethnic, and genealogical origin.

4. *[Insert paragraph #4 from the choices in the following section that most fits your situation. Medical reasons from your doctor are the best choice if you have that option.]*

5. That the release of confidential information would be in the best interests of the Adoptee.

6. That Petitioner formally waives any rights to confidentiality relating to this adoption.

7. That Petitioner hereby requests that the Court open the adoption file and provide the requested information directly to Petitioner or as a last alternative that the Court appoints a Confidential Intermediary to contact the other parties to secure Waivers of Confidentiality.

WHEREFORE, Petitioner *[YOUR NAME]* prays that this Honorable Court will make an order directing the Clerk of the Court to prepare, certify and deliver to the Petitioner a copy of *[her/his]* original identifying adoption records for compelling needs and good cause showing and for such other and further relief as the Court may deem just and proper.

Respectfully submitted this _____ day of _____, 20____ .

By:_____
Name
Address
City, state, zip
Phone
Petitioner Pro Se

VERIFICATION AND ACKNOWLEDGEMENT

STATE OF *[state where notarized]*)
)ss.
COUNTY OF *[county where notarized]*)

THE ABOVE NAMED PETITIONER, *[your name]*, personally appeared before me, a Notary Public, on the date above-written, and having been duly sworn upon oath acknowledged to me that *[she/he]* was the person that had executed the foregoing VERIFIED PETITION FOR ACCESS TO SEALED ADOPTION RECORDS, having read and understood it, and knowing the contents thereof to be true and correct, based upon *[his/her]* personal knowledge, and swearing to the truth thereof, and having voluntarily subscribed *[his/her]* name thereto intending to be bound thereby.

_____
Notary Public

Residing at: _____

My Commission Expires:_____

Petition Sentence Choices

2. That Petitioner's adoption was handled by *[attorney or agency name]* at *[attorney or agency street]*, *[attorney or agency city, state and zip)*

2. That Petitioner does not know what agency or attorney handled the adoption.

4. That the adoptee has a medical need for health information of genetic significance that may affect *[his/her]* physical or emotional mental health. A letter from Petitioner's doctor is attached as Exhibit C.

4. That the adoptee has children and believes that *[he/she]* has a responsibility to know about *[his/her]* natural family's medical and genealogical background for *[his/her]* family.

4. That the adoptee is contemplating a future with children and believes that *[he/she]* has a responsibility to know about *[his/her]* natural family's medical and genealogical background for *[his/her]* family.

Affidavit Accompanying Verified Petition

This Affidavit is the same as the previous Affidavit shown in this book with the exception of the title of the document being different in the heading. Here is the heading that you should use for **this** Affidavit. This is the Affidavit that must accompany the Petition. Read the instructions from the first Affidavit and follow them exactly the same for this one. The Certificate of Mailing on the following page goes after this completed Affidavit.

Always double-space your documents where it is shown on these examples. Chose one of the following sentences to insert into your Affidavit where indicated on the next page.

Affidavit Sentence Choices

3. My adoption was handled by *(name of agency or attorney)*.

3. I do not know the name of the agency or attorney who handled my adoption.

4. I have a medical need for health information of genetic significance that may affect my physical or mental health. A letter from my physician is attached. *[Medical reasons from your doctor are the best choice if you have that option.]*

4. I am contemplating a future with children and believe that I have a responsibility to know about my natural family's medical and genealogical background for my family.

4. I have children and believe that I have a responsibility to know about my natural family's medical and genealogical background for my family.

82

YOUR NAME
Your Street
Your City, State and zip
Your area code and phone number
Petitioner Pro Se

IN THE (*Your Court*) COURT OF THE

STATE OF *STATE* IN AND FOR THE COUNTY OF *COUNTY*

YOUR NAME,	) CASE NO.
	) Adoption File No._____
	) Department:
Petitioner.	)

AFFIDAVIT ACCOMPANYING VERIFIED PETITION
FOR ACCESS TO SEALED ADOPTION RECORDS

STATE OF *[your state]*   )
) SS.
COUNTY OF *[your county]*   )

I, *[YOUR NAME]*, being first duly sworn, upon my oath do solemnly swear under penalty of perjury that:

1. I am a resident of *[county]* County. My address is *[street]*, *[city]*, *[state]* *[zip]* and my phone number is *[telephone]*.

2. I am a mature adult adoptee and was born on *[birth date]* at *[birth hospital]* Hospital in *[city]*, *[state]*, *[county]* County and was adopted by *[adoptive father]* and *[adoptive mother]* and they gave me the name of *[adoption name]*.

3. *[Insert paragraph #3 from the choices following this Affidavit that most fits your situation.]*

4. *[Insert paragraph #4 from the choices following this Affidavit that most fits your situation.]*

5. I give full and legal permission to release my present identity and whereabouts as given above to my immediate birth family effective for 99 years, even after my death.

83

6. I authorize the administrator and the administrator's designees to inspect all vital statistic records, court records, and agency records, including confidential records, relating to my birth, marriage, and divorce (as applicable) to the birth and death of any sibling or adoption of myself.

7. I believe that I have good cause to inspect the contents of my birth records in their entirety.

DATED this _____ day of _____, 20____.

_____
[type your name here]

SUBSCRIBED and SWORN to before me
this _____ day of _____, 20___

_____
NOTARY PUBLIC
My Commission Expires: _____

CERTIFICATE OF MAILING

I HEREBY CERTIFY that on the _____ day of
_____, 20____, I served a true and
correct copy of the foregoing NOTICE, VERIFIED PETITION
FOR ACCESS TO SEALED ADOPTION RECORDS, and AFFIDAVIT
ACCOMPANYING VERIFIED PETITION FOR ACCESS TO SEALED
ADOPTION RECORDS by depositing a copy of the same in the
United States mail via First Class Mail, postage
prepaid, addressed as follows:

*(Bureau of vital statistics name found in this book. Do
not type this line)*

address
city, state, zip

[attorney or agency name]
[attorney or agency street]
[attorney or agency city, state and zip)

_____
[type your name here]

*(only include addresses if applicable and do not type
this italicized line)*

Order on Petition

Double-space where shown. If the Judge grants your Petition you will then need to give the ORDER to the clerk for the Judge's signature. Do **not** file this Order **unless** the Judge grants your Petition. Ask the clerk how many copies they need. After the Judge signs it and it is sent to you, this is the paper that you will take with you to get your records opened. Mail copies of this Order to everyone listed on the Certificate of Mailing. If the Judge does NOT grant your Petition, the Court will draft its own Order of Denial. If you have an Order granting your Petition, the Court may also require nominal fees from you for the search and production of documents, etc.

Order Sentence Choices

Chose one of the following sentences to insert into your Order where indicated on the next page.

```
(she or he) has a medical need for health

information of genetic significance that may affect

(his or her) physical or mental health.

(she or he) has children and (she or he) has a

responsibility to know about (his or her) natural

family's medical and genealogical background for

(his or her) family.

(she or he) is contemplating a future with children

and has a responsibility to know about (his or her)

natural family's medical and genealogical

background for (his or her) family.
```

YOUR NAME
Your Street
Your City, State and zip
Your area code and phone number
Petitioner Pro Se

IN THE *ADOPTION* COURT OF THE

STATE OF *STATE* IN AND FOR THE COUNTY OF *COUNTY*

_____
)
YOUR NAME,   ) CASE NO.
) Adoption File No._____
) Department:
          Petitioner.   )
_____)

ORDER ON VERIFIED PETITION FOR ACCESS TO

SEALED ADOPTION RECORDS

  The Verified Petition For Access to Sealed Adoption
Records of the above-named child having been filed in this
Court, and notice having been given to necessary parties, NOW,
and upon all the papers and proceedings herein, it is hereby
ORDERED that the Verified Petition For Access to Sealed
Adoption Records is GRANTED and that *YOUR NAME* shall be given
access to sealed identifying adoption records for good cause
showing on the grounds that *[Type in here one of the three*
options listed on the previous page. It should be the same as
the choice you made in the Petition only with this selections
wording.]

  DATED this _____ day of _____, 20____.

                              _____
                                        PRESIDING JUDGE

87

Finished Example

JANE DOE
100 Any Street
Las Vegas, Nevada 89000
702-555-5555
Petitioner Pro Se

IN THE 1ST DISTRICT COURT OF THE

STATE OF NEVADA IN AND FOR THE COUNTY OF CLARK

JANE DOE	) CASE NO.:
	) Adoption File No.:
Petitioner.	) Department:

NOTICE OF VERIFIED PETITION TO UNSEAL ADOPTION RECORDS

YOU AND EACH OF YOU WILL PLEASE TAKE NOTICE that the undersigned will bring the Verified Petition To Unseal Adoption Records filed on _____, 20___, before the above-entitled Court on the _____day of _____, 20___, at the hour of _____ ___.m. of said day, in Department _____ of said Court.

DATED this _____ day of _____, 20____.

By: _____
    JANE DOE
    100 Any Street
    Las Vegas, Nevada 89000
    702-555-5555
    Petitioner Pro Se

[Note: This Notice of Petition for Access to Sealed Adoption Records is served upon you as required by law. You are not required to appear or to respond. However, should you fail to appear or respond on or before the date set forth in Paragraph 1, it will be assumed you do not object to the relief requested. You may have an attorney appear for you.]

JANE DOE
100 Any Street
Las Vegas, Nevada 89000
702-555-5555
Petitioner Pro Se

IN THE 1ST DISTRICT COURT OF THE

STATE OF NEVADA IN AND FOR THE COUNTY OF CLARK

JANE DOE	) CASE NO.:
	) Adoption File No.:
	) Department:
Petitioner.	)
	)

VERIFIED PETITION FOR ACCESS TO SEALED ADOPTION RECORDS

COMES NOW JANE DOE, Petitioner Pro Se, and respectfully petitions the Court to authorize the Clerk of the Court to allow the Petitioner access to all her adoption and birth-record identifying information pursuant to Nevada Revised Statutes § NRS 127.140 for good cause showing as follows:

1. That Petitioner Jane Doe is the adoptee in this case and is now a mature adult who was born July 4, 1960 in Las Vegas, Nevada and was adopted by James Doe and Marion Doe. A copy of Petitioner's birth certificate is attached as Exhibit A and proof of current address and legal identification as Exhibit B.

2. That Petitioner does not know what agency or attorney handled the adoption.

3. That the adoptee has a strong and healthy desire and curiosity to have access to records concerning the identity of her biological parents, biological heritage, religious, genetic, ethnic, and genealogical origin.

4. That the adoptee has a medical need for health information of genetic significance that may affect her physical or

emotional mental health. A letter from Petitioner's doctor is attached as Exhibit C.

5. That the release of confidential information would be in the best interests of the Adoptee.

6. That Petitioner formally waives any rights to confidentiality relating to this adoption.

7. That Petitioner hereby requests that the Court open the adoption file and provide the requested information directly to Petitioner or as a last alternative that the Court appoints a Confidential Intermediary to contact the other parties to secure Waivers of Confidentiality.

WHEREFORE, Petitioner Jane Doe prays that this Honorable Court will make an order directing the Clerk of the Court to prepare, certify and deliver to the Petitioner a copy of her original identifying adoption records for compelling needs and good cause showing and for such other and further relief as the Court may deem just and proper.

Respectfully submitted this _____ day of _____, 20____ .

By: _____
JANE DOE
100 Any Street
Las Vegas, Nevada 89000
702-555-5555
Petitioner Pro Se

VERIFICATION AND ACKNOWLEDGEMENT

STATE OF NEVADA   )
)ss.
COUNTY OF CLARK   ) .

       THE ABOVE NAMED PETITIONER, Jane Doe, personally appeared before me, a Notary Public, on the date above-written, and having been duly sworn upon oath acknowledged to me that she was the person that had executed the foregoing VERIFIED PETITION FOR ACCESS TO SEALED ADOPTION RECORDS, having read and understood it, and knowing the contents thereof to be true and correct, based upon her personal knowledge, and swearing to the truth thereof, and having voluntarily subscribed her name thereto intending to be bound thereby.

_____

Notary Public

Residing at: _____

My Commission Expires:_____

91

JANE DOE
100 Any Street
Las Vegas, Nevada 89000
702-555-5555
Petitioner Pro Se

IN THE 1ST DISTRICT COURT OF THE

STATE OF NEVADA IN AND FOR THE COUNTY OF CLARK

JANE DOE	)
	) CASE NO.:
	) Adoption File No.:
	) Department:
Petitioner.	)

**AFFIDAVIT ACCOMPANYING VERIFIED PETITION
FOR ACCESS TO SEALED ADOPTION RECORDS**

STATE OF NEVADA	)
	)ss.
COUNTY OF CLARK	)

I, Jane Doe, being first duly sworn, upon my oath do solemnly swear under penalty of perjury that:

1. I am a resident of Clark County. My address is 100 Any Street, Las Vegas, Nevada 89000 and my phone number is 702-555-5555.

2. I am a mature adult adoptee and was born on July 4, 1960 at University Medical Hospital in Las Vegas, Nevada, Clark County and was adopted by James Doe and Marion Doe and they gave me the name of Jane Doe.

3. I do not know the name of the agency or attorney who handled my adoption.

4. I have a medical need for health information of genetic significance that may affect my physical or mental health. A letter from my physician is attached.5. I give full and legal

92

permission to release my present identity and whereabouts as given above to my immediate birth family effective for 99 years, even after my death.

6. I authorize the administrator and the administrator's designees to inspect all vital statistic records, court records, and agency records, including confidential records, relating to my birth, marriage, and divorce (as applicable) to the birth and death of any sibling or adoption of myself.

7. I believe that I have good cause to inspect the contents of my birth records in their entirety.

DATED this _____ day of _____, 20____ .

_____
JANE DOE

SUBSCRIBED and SWORN to before me
this _____ day of _____, 20___

_____
NOTARY PUBLIC
My Commission Expires: _____

CERTIFICATE OF MAILING

I HEREBY CERTIFY that on the _____ day of _____, 20____, I served a true and correct copy of the foregoing NOTICE, VERIFIED PETITION FOR ACCESS TO SEALED ADOPTION RECORDS, and AFFIDAVIT ACCOMPANYING VERIFIED PETITION FOR ACCESS TO SEALED ADOPTION RECORDS by depositing a copy of the same in the United States mail via First Class Mail, postage prepaid, addressed as follows:

Nevada Office of Vital Records and Statistics
Capitol Complex
505 East King St., Room 102
Carson City, NV 89701-4749

_____
JANE DOE

JANE DOE
100 Any Street
Las Vegas, Nevada 89000
702-555-5555
Petitioner Pro Se

IN THE 1ST DISTRICT COURT OF THE

STATE OF NEVADA IN AND FOR THE COUNTY OF CLARK

JANE DOE	)
	) CASE NO.:
	) Adoption File No.:
	) Department:
Petitioner.	)
	)

ORDER ON VERIFIED PETITION FOR ACCESS TO

SEALED ADOPTION RECORDS

The Verified Petition For Access to Sealed Adoption
Records of the above-named child having been filed in this
Court, and notice having been given to necessary parties, NOW,
and upon all the papers and proceedings herein, it is hereby
ORDERED that the Verified Petition For Access to Sealed
Adoption Records is GRANTED and that JANE DOE shall be given
access to sealed identifying adoption records for good cause
showing on the grounds that she has a medical need for health
information of genetic significance that may affect her
physical or mental health.

DATED this _____ day of _____, 20____.

_____
PRESIDING JUDGE

Search Angels

There are people willing to do research either nationwide or in their own and/or nearby states. Some will go to libraries and courthouses and personally check records for birth families. Most will not charge for their time, but some may want reimbursement for out of pocket expenses such as long-distance calls, gas if they have to travel long distances, or for the cost of certified copies. These good people are "Search Angels." There is also a group called Volunteer Search network where you can register for "cost only" search help at: vsn.org/

Before contacting them, be sure to have registered at the I.S.R.R. listed in the Getting Started section of this book. It could lead to a match and would prevent wasting their time as well as yours. Most search angels will require this before they help anyway. Having your Non-Id information ahead of time is also helpful in locating your birth family.

Generally, these "Angels" are not professionals. So please understand that they are usually part of the adoption triad or relatives themselves and just want to help where they can. Please do not ask Search Angels to make contact if they find your information. This is not their responsibility and can have legal consequences for both of you.

You will need access to a computer. If you do not have one, the library has computers you can use, or you can pay for computer time at places such as Kinko's. You will also need an email account to contact most of these people. If you need one, Yahoo would be the best free email program to access because it also allows you use their groups for registration, as you will see in the next section.

Some search angels will require you to mention you found their name in this book before they will help so be sure to mention it so they will know how you found them. Put

"Adoption Records Handbook" in the subject line of your emails.

Chris Graves lives in California and limits his searches to those born in California. He does California birth/death index, marriage index 1949-1985, Nevada marriage index, US Post Office box holders by name and location as well as many other indexes and publications. It is helpful for the adoptee to have his/her NonID before contact, as well as the State and Local numbers on the birth certificate. He does not charge a fee. Email: caliron@cwnet.com

Marge Smith is located in NE Ohio. She can search the Ohio birth index and marriage index. She will do footwork in the Cleveland/NE Ohio area and knows her way around the courthouses, library, and whatever is needed in the Ohio area. E-Mail: wow494949@yahoo.com

Lezli Adams can help in Ohio, Kentucky, and a little in Southern Indiana. She has Kentucky and Ohio Birth Indexes, has been an adoption search angel since 1999, and has reunited hundreds of people over the years. Email: lezliadams@insightbb.com

Adrienne E. Wojtowicz, 4503 N. Spyglass Cr., Wichita, Ks 67226. 316-636-5190. She does searches in all states, at no charge. She's a birth mother and is also available for support if anyone just needs to talk. Email: Hearts121@sbcglobal.net

Susan lives in Germany and speaks the language. Many GI-Babies were adopted in Germany by American military families and now seek information on their birth families. She has found several matches and never charges fees, not even for her phone calls. If needed, German government fees are paid by the searcher directly to their offices. Email: RSPauls@aol.com

Cherrie can cover IN, WI, and IL. Resources: Access to ancestry.com, classmates.com, and also certain D.M.V. for IL and Cedar Lake, Indiana. Email: rogersc490@aol.com

Lisa V. lives in the Orange County, CA. area. She is willing to purchase any database she can to help. She has internet access and lives in the middle of many different cities. Irvine, Tustin, Santa Ana, Newport Beach, Laguna area, Yorba Linda. She is minutes away from the county courthouse of Santa Ana. Email: ocsearchangel@yahoo.com

Ginger Farrow has been co-founder of a search and support group based in Delaware for over 20 years and Delaware is her state of expertise. She has old Polk City, Delaware city directories and can direct people to groups who will help in every state as well as some foreign countries. She also does searches for Black Market babies in the Veil Hospital in Middletown, DE with reference to Dr. Jerome Niles. Ginger Farrow, P.O.Box 181, Bear, DE 19701-0181. Email: SearchDe@aol.com

Pamela Hewitt searches the areas of St. Clair, Macomb, and Sanilac counties in Michigan. She does not charge for her services except for gas and then only if she has to travel some distance to get to a library or for court records. Email: mzfitkid@comcast.net

Sandee Hardy does searches in the Kinston, NC (Lenoir County) area with Register of Deeds Office, Library etc. She does not charge unless it is for copies. Email: SandeeBeaches94@Yahoo.com

Susan Messina searches Florida, New York and Texas. She has completed many reunions and says the feeling is worth more than gold. Email: smes565845@aol.com

Loretta lives in Charlotte, NC and is willing to help search for anyone seeking information in Mecklenburg County and some for Guilford and Durham Counties. She does not charge for her time, but likes to be reimbursed for out of pocket expenses if any. Her major frustration comes from those that post, leave their contact information, move and do not update their contact info. She spends more time looking for the poster than she does the one that posts. Email: Nyclore@aol.com

Ellen Bishop can search in Rapid City, SD and vicinity. Email: Ellenb7580@aol.com

Mike Acton Because of recent legislation in the UK, adoption searches have been taken out of the hands of independent researchers. Only government appointed Adoption Search Agencies are allowed to see related searches through to completion. These ASA's are costly to set up; therefore out of reach of Search Angels. However, he can help by giving information regarding the process within the law. He specializes on preWW2 searches. Email: michaelacton587@msn.com

Teri can do yearbook look-ups for Scottsdale High School in Scottsdale, Arizona for the years of 1956 through 1960. Email: tabrown@yahoo.com The "o" in brown is a zero.

Barbara Campbell has been doing searches in South Carolina for over 10 years. You can reach her at 864-833-4310. Email: Barbara_from_sc@yahoo.com

Kim Wells is a search angel for the state of VA. She does leg work in the Tidewater area: Norfolk, Portsmouth, Chesapeake, & Virginia Beach. She never charges to search but that could change with the price of gas climbing, but for gas only. She often finds a birth last name, and from there takes the non-id and searches marriages and from that one document, she can fill in those "blanks" in the non-id. Email: kwells64@cox.net

Cindy Schwei of Minnesota has been a volunteer with EMLA since 2005 and can help with Minnesota searches except for medical necessities when she will search anywhere. She charges only if she has to travel outside the metro area of Minneapolis and St. Paul for gas or if she needs a certified document. Email: schw0273@gmail.com

Donna M. can search Spartenburg, S.C., Duncan, S.C., Woodruff, S.C., and the surrounding area. She has unlimited local and long distance and has a home office with a fax. Does not charge fees. Email: DonnaMer66@yahoo.com

Suzanne Morava searches in Texas and Oklahoma and will only charge for gas, certified certificates, and long distance phone calls. She is a professional skip tracer so you must mention you found her name in this book in order to not be charged her normal hourly rates. Email: morava@sbcglobal.net

Lori Ewert-Sanders, an adoptee who has found her birth families. She is actually a children's librarian in California, but she searches during her free time. She is tenacious and unrelenting: which are two of the most important traits needed by a search angel. She has access to several databases, and has an extremely high success rate. She prefers to do her research mainly in California, but she can do other states as well. Email: Ithakasearch@sbcglobal.net

Joyce Finch is a free California Search Angel and does mostly California searches. If you live in another state and you were born in California, she does that. Email: joycef14@sbcglobal.net

Lucinda Martin can search most of Northern Utah. She is located in the Box Elder county area and is willing to help in any part of Utah. She has access to libraries, newspapers, city halls, plus many friends always willing to help. Email: luscorpio1967@hotmail.com

Jeanette does searches in New Jersey and can check libraries and courthouses, etc. in northern New Jersey. She also does phone directories, yearbooks, and has gone to the high schools in various areas with her searches. Email: jeanette.edler@comcast.net

Kim Johnston searches primarily in Texas and will search all the counties. She searches mostly online with ancestry, yearbooks and goes to the Dallas Library when needed. She does not charge except for out-of-pocket expenses. Email: rjkj1118@aol.com

Leslie lives in Eugene, Oregon (Lane County) and can also research (Polk) City. She has directories for almost every city in Oregon. Leslie has Directories for about any city in Oregon. (at the University of Oregon), Oregon Marriage, Divorce and Death Index. She is a member at Ancestry. Com, has access to

Ancestry.com (SSDI, etc), Netdetectives and Oregon database (dmv-type, searchable). Email: bfamilysearcher@aol.com

Dawn is an adoption reunification specialist who *will* charge for her services, but will occasionally do pro bono searches. She searches open book states and the five boroughs of NYC. She searches birth indexes, the death index, old directories, and Ellis Island. If you hire her she requires your registration in the New York State adoption registry and the I.S.R.R. Email: katzeyez70@yahoo.com

Aunt Patty prefers to work on searches in New York but will assist where she's needed. She is a crisis intervention counselor of women specializing in what she calls "damage control" when reunions have gone bad or gotten off to a bad start. Email: lovesdonna2@yahoo.com

Online Groups & Registries

The internet has a vast number of resources and a multitude of people willing to help as well as offer lots of support and suggestions to assist you in your search. The more groups and registries that you join, the better your odds will be in finding a match.

For most of these groups, you will need a Yahoo ID name in order to join them. Yahoo offers free email and this is where you will sign up. Your Yahoo user name will be your ID to join groups. There are many more than are listed here but these seem to have the most members. You can also do more searches for other groups on adoption related topics.

groups.yahoo.com/group/FloridaSearchAngels/
groups.yahoo.com/group/OfTheWombAndOfTheHeart
groups.yahoo.com/group/ky-adoptions/
groups.yahoo.com/group/newmexico
groups.yahoo.com/group/SoCarolinaAdoptions
groups.yahoo.com/group/AdoptionSearchandSupport
groups.yahoo.com/group/Adoption-Search-Angels
groups.yahoo.com/group/VASearch
groups.yahoo.com/group/parr (PA)
groups.yahoo.com/group/COregistry
groups.yahoo.com/group/FLORIDA-AdopteesSearching
groups.yahoo.com/group/LookinginOntario
groups.yahoo.com/group/OAR-BirthName-Registry
groups.yahoo.com/group/Finding-in-Florida
groups.yahoo.com/group/ReunitingMinnesota
groups.yahoo.com/group/CaliforniaAdoptees
groups.yahoo.com/group/QichunHubeiPRC China
groups.yahoo.com/group/NewYorkLibertyAngels
groups.yahoo.com/group/regday
groups.yahoo.com/group/BoothBabyAdoptionRegistry
groups.yahoo.com/group/FallingLeavesRegistry
groups.yahoo.com/group/GuatemalaAdopt_SiblingRegistry
groups.yahoo.com/group/adoptionregistrymagazine

groups.yahoo.com/group/SearchingRegistry
groups.yahoo.com/group/Oklahoma_Registry
groups.yahoo.com/group/Missouri_Adoption_Registry
groups.yahoo.com/group/EffectiveAdoptionRegistry
groups.yahoo.com/group/michiganadoptions
groups.yahoo.com/group/INAdoption
groups.yahoo.com/group/Adoption-Reunion-Registry
groups.yahoo.com/group/MichiganFamilyTiesAdoptionSearch
groups.yahoo.com/group/BSNR2
groups.yahoo.com/group/theregistry 2600 members
groups.yahoo.com/group/Angels-Blessing-Search-Support
groups.yahoo.com/group/adoption-search-reunions
groups.yahoo.com/group/SoaringAngels
groups.yahoo.com/group/togetheragain

Other registries

members.aol.com/Espaura/MAadopt.html
    Massachusetts Registry
www.icareregistry.com/register/   Wisconsin
www.geocities.com/Heartland/Flats/9073/regentry.html
    Tennessee
www.txcare.org/index.shtml   Texas
www.worldwidetracers.com/adoption/
registry.adoption.com/
www.adoptionregistry.us/
www.findme.org/index.cfm?fuseaction=Main
www.arvinpublications.com/registry.html
www.adopting.org/adoptions/free-national-world-adoption
-reunion-registries.html
www.dss.mo.gov/cd/adopt/adoir.htm   Missouri
www.idph.state.il.us/vitalrecords/adoptioninfo.htm Illinois
www.canadianadopteesregistry.org/disc_registrys.html
    Canada
www.gsadoptionregistry.com/   National
bodhipines.com/6nations/   Iroquois Nation Registry
www.geocities.com/Heartland/Acres/9942/registry.html
adoptflorida.com/Reunion-Registry.htm   Florida
www.healthandwelfare.idaho.gov/_Rainbow/Documents/fa
milies/Adoption%20Registry%20Form.pdf   Idaho
www.health.state.mn.us/divs/chs/registry/reginst.htm
    MN Father's Adoption Registry

www.longlostpeople.com/
www.geocities.com/geoadopt/registry/registry.html
    All States
www.metroreunionregistry.org/   International Registry
www.adopteeconnect.com/p/a/1035//aq/sa//r/60/10
    NC
www.whentheboughbreaks.net/
www.adoption-free-search.org/ Emergency Medical
    Locators
adoptionrecords.org/searchbirthday.html
100megsfree3.com/levgen/data.html
www.eboards4all.com/343402/
registry.adoption.com/advanced_search.php?action=dates
www.bmom.net/
www.iwasadopted.com   International Registry
Canada, British Columbia's Adoption Reunion Registry:
www.adoptionreunion.net
World Wide Registry:
www.geocities.com/Heartland/Estates/5206/form.html
Black Market Adoptees Registry:
www.geocities.com/Heartland/Garden/2313/
Merry-Go-Round International Adoption Search Registry:
www.geocities.com/Heartland/Garden /1145/post

SAFE ONLINE ADOPTION REGISTRIES (SOAR)

- Adoption Search And Find Registry:
  www.geocities.com/Heartland/Ridge/2755
- Alabamians Working for Adoption Reform and
  Education: www.alabama-adoption.org
- Arkansas Adoption Connection:
  www.arkansasadoption.com
- The Cole Baby Registry:
  www.angelfire.com/fl2/colebaby/blank.html
- Indiana Searching:
  www.geocities.com/heartland/park/3560
- Kayhh's adoption registry:
  www.geocities.com/Heartland/8529/adopt/1ADreg
- Lost n Found Adoption Registry:
  www.niwot.net/adopt

Adoption Agencies

The following adoption agencies have been supportive of open adoption records in the past and hopefully still are. If you were born at, or gave birth at, any agencies on this list, you may be able to get information from them. This information generously provided by Joe Soll at: www.adoptioncrossroads.org/

Massachusetts Dept of Social Services
24 Farnsworth Street
Boston, MA 02210
617-727-0900

Children's Aid & Adopt Soc of NJ
575 Main Street
Hackensack, NJ 07601
201-487-2022

Catholic Charities
PO Box 358
Millington, NJ 07946
908-604-69892

Downey Side
371 7th Avenue
Hudson Room
New York, NY 10001
212-629-8599

McMahon Services for Children
225 East 45th Street
New York, NY 10017
212-972-7070

Spence-Chapin
6 East 94th Street
New York, NY 10128
212-369-0300

Family Services of Westchester
One Summit Avenue
White Plains, NY 10606
914-948-8004

Help Us Regain the Children
235 Dover Street
Brooklyn, NY 11235
718-332-0860

The Adoption Agency
76 Rittenhouse Place
Ardmore, PA 19003
215-642-7200

Orphan Foundation of America,
1500 MA Avenue NW, Suite 448
Washington DC 20005
202-861-0762

Associated Catholic Charities
19 W Franklin Street, 2nd Floor
Baltimore, MD 21201
301-659-4050

Children's Home Society of Virginia
4200 Firzhugh Avenue
Richmond, VA 23230
804-353-0191

Children's Home Society of West Virginia
1145 Greenbrier Street
Charleston, WV 25311
304-346-0795

Family & Child Services
5201 Airport Hiway
Birmingham, AL 35213
205-595-3621

Americans for African Adoptions
8910 Timberwood Drive
Indianapolis, IN 46234
317-271-4567

The OPTIONS Alliance
2218 Cabrillo Avenue
Torrance, CA 90501
310-212-5814

PACT: An Adoption Alliance
3450 Sacramento Street, Suite 239
San Francisco, CA 94118
415-221-6957

Holt International Children's Services,
PO Box 2880
Eugene, OR 97402
Email: laurah@holtintl.org
541-687-2202

Casey Family Program,
200 Elliott Ave. W. #110
Seattle, WA 98119
206-286-4450

Child Welfare Society
PO Box 2539
Johannesburg, South Africa 2000

Online Court Locations

Alabama
www.alacourt.gov/JudicialCircuits.aspx

Alaska
www.state.ak.us/courts/courtdir.htm

Arizona
www.arizonasearch.org/superiorcourts.html

California
www.courtinfo.ca.gov/courts/find.htm

Arkansas
courts.state.ar.us/index.cfm

Colorado
www.courts.state.co.us

Connecticut
www.jud.ct.gov

Delaware
courts.delaware.gov

District of Columbia
www.dccourts.gov/dccourts/index.jsp

Florida
www.flcourts.org

Georgia
www.georgiacourts.org

Hawaii
www.courts.state.hi.us/index.jsp

Idaho
www.isc.idaho.gov

Illinois
www.state.il.us/court

Indiana
www.in.gov/judiciary

Iowa
www.judicial.state.ia.us

Kansas
www.kscourts.org

Kentucky
courts.ky.gov

Louisiana
www.findlaw.com/11stategov/la/courts.html

Maine
www.courts.state.me.us/maine_courts/findacourt.html

Maryland
www.courts.state.md.us

Massachusetts
www.mass.gov/courts/courtsandjudges/courts/index.html

Michigan
courts.michigan.gov

Minnesota
www.mncourts.gov/default.aspx

Mississippi
www.mssc.state.ms.us

Missouri
www.courts.mo.gov

Montana
www.montanacourts.org

Nebraska
www.supremecourt.ne.gov

Nevada
www.nvsupremecourt.us/info/nvcourts

New Hampshire
www.courts.state.nh.us/courtlocations/index.htm

New Jersey
www.judiciary.state.nj.us

New Mexico
www.nmcourts.gov/othercourts.html

New York
www.courts.state.ny.us/courts

North Carolina
www.nccourts.org/Courts/Default.asp

North Dakota
www.ndcourts.com/court/courts.htm

Ohio
www.ohiojudges.org/index.cfm?PageID=64C16230-2FAD-4EE3-99C37E40B578079B

Oklahoma
www.oscn.net/applications/oscn/start.asp?viewType=COURTS

Oregon
www.ojd.state.or.us/courts/index.htm

Pennsylvania
www.courts.state.pa.us/Index/UJS/indexujs.asp

Rhode Island
www.courts.ri.gov

South Carolina
www.judicial.state.sc.us

South Dakota
www.50states.com/south_dakota/state_courts.htm

Tennessee
www.govengine.com/statecourts/tennessee.html

Texas
www.megalaw.com/tx/txcourts.php

Utah
www.utcourts.gov/directory

Vermont
www.vermontjudiciary.org/Resources/directions.htm

Virginia
www.courts.state.va.us/rule115.html

Washington
www.courts.wa.gov/court_dir/

West Virginia
www.state.wv.us/wvsca/wvsystem.htm

Wisconsin
www.wicourts.gov/contact/ccsites.htm

Wisconsin Tribal Courts
www.judicare.org/trcts.html

Wyoming
courts.state.wy.us

Health Departments

Copies of legal documents should be submitted to the vital records office in the city/state where the person was born or the city/state where the mother resided at the time of birth. These listings and other offices within the same state can be found online at the National Center for Health Statistics at: www.cdc.gov/nchs/howto/w2w/w2wel com.htm

Alabama Vital Records
State Department of Public Health
P.O. Box 5625
Montgomery, AL 36103-5625

Alaska Department of Health and Social Services
Bureau of Vital Statistics
5441 Commercial Boulevard
Juneau, AK 99801

Office of Vital Records
Arizona Department of Health Services
P.O. Box 3887
Phoenix, AZ 85030-3887

Arkansas Vital Records H-44
4815 West Markham
Little Rock, AR 72205

Office of Vital Records
California Department of Public Health
MS: 5103
P.O. Box 997410
Sacramento, CA 95899-7410

Vital Records Section
Colorado Department of Public Health and Environment
4300 Cherry Creek Drive South
HSVRD-VS-A1
Denver, CO 80246-1530

Connecticut State Vital Records
Department of Public Health
410 Capitol Ave, MS #11 VRS
Hartford, CT 06134

Delaware Office of Vital Statistics
Division of Public Health
417 Federal Street
Dover, DE 19901

District of Columbia
Vital Records Division
825 North Capitol Street NE
Washington, DC 20002

Florida Department of Health
Office of Vital Statistics
P.O. Box 210
1217 Pearl Street
Jacksonville, FL 32231-0042

Georgia Department of Human Resources
Vital Records
2600 Skyland Drive, NE
Atlanta, GA 30319-3640

Hawaii State Department of Health
Office of Health Status Monitoring
Vital Records Section
P.O. Box 3378
Honolulu, HI 96801-9984

Idaho Vital Statistics Unit
Bureau of Health Policy and Vital Statistics
P.O. Box 83720
Boise, ID 83720-0036

Division of Vital Records
Illinois Department of Public Health
605 West Jefferson Street
Springfield, IL 62702-5097

Vital Records
Indiana State Department of Health
P.O. Box 7125
Indianapolis, IN 46206-7125

Iowa Department of Public Health
Bureau of Vital Records
Lucas Office Building
321 East 12th Street
Des Moines, IA 50319-0075

Office of Vital Statistics
Curtis State Office Building
1000 SW Jackson Street, Suite 120
Topeka, **Kansas** 66612-2221

Kentucky Office of Vital Statistics
Department for Health Services
275 East Main Street
Frankfort, KY 40621

Louisiana Office of Public Health
Vital Records Registry
P.O. Box 60630
New Orleans, LA 70160

Office of Vital Records
Maine Department of Human Services
244 Water Street
#11 State House Station
Augusta, ME 04333-0011

Maryland Division of Vital Records
Department of Health
6550 Reisterstown Road
P.O. Box 68760
Baltimore, MD 21215-0020

Massachusetts Registry of Vital Records and Statistics
150 Mount Vernon Street, 1st Floor
Dorchester, MA 02125-3105

Vital Records Request
P.O. Box 30721
Lansing, **Michigan** 48909

Office of the State Registrar
Minnesota Department of Health
P.O. Box 64882
St Paul, MN 55164-0082

Mississippi Vital Records
State Department of Health
P.O. Box 1700
Jackson, MS 39215-1700

Missouri Department of Health
Bureau of Vital Records
930 Wildwood
P.O. Box 570
Jefferson City, MO 65102-0570

Office of Vital Statistics
Montana Department of Public Health and Human Services
111 N Sanders, Room 209
P.O. Box 4210
Helena, MT 59604

Nebraska Vital Records
1033 O Street, Suite 130
P.O. Box 95065
Lincoln, NE 68509-5065

Nevada Office of Vital Records and Statistics
Capitol Complex
505 East King Street, Room 102
Carson City, NV 89701-4749

New Hampshire Division of Vital Records Administration
Archives Building
71 South Fruit Street
Concord, NH 03301-2410

Bureau of Vital Statistics
New Jersey Department of Health
P. O. Box 370
Trenton, NJ 08625-0370

New Mexico Vital Records
P.O. Box 26110
Santa Fe, NM 87502

For all New York except New York City
New York Certification Unit
Vital Records Section, 2nd Floor
800 North Pearl Street
Menands, NY 12204

Office of Vital Records
New York City Department of Health and Mental Hygiene
125 Worth St, CN4, Room 133
New York, NY 10013-4090

North Carolina Vital Records
1903 Mail Service Center
Raleigh, NC 27699-1903

North Dakota Department of Health
Division of Vital Records
600 East Boulevard Avenue, Department 301
Bismarck, ND 58505-0200

Vital Statistics
Ohio Department of Health
246 North High Street, 1st Floor
Columbus, OH 43216

Vital Records Service
State Department of Health
1000 Northeast 10th Street
Oklahoma City, OK 73117

Oregon Vital Records
P.O. Box 14050
Portland, OR 97293-0050

Pennsylvania Division of Vital Records
ATTN: Birth Unit
101 South Mercer Street
Central Building, Room 401
P.O. Box 1528
New Castle, PA 16103

Office of Vital Records
Rhode Island Department of Health
3 Capitol Hill, Room 101
Providence, RI 02908-5097

Office of Vital Records
South Carolina DHEC
2600 Bull Street
Columbia, SC 29201

South Dakota Vital Records
State Department of Health
207 East Missouri Avenue, Suite 1-A
Pierre, SD 57501

Tennessee Vital Records
Central Services Building
421 5th Avenue, North
Nashville, TN 37247

Bureau of Vital Statistics
Texas Department of Health
P.O. Box 12040
Austin, TX 78711-2040

Office of Vital Records
Utah Department of Health
288 North 1460 West
P.O. Box 141012
Salt Lake City, UT 84114-1012

Vermont Department of Health
Vital Records Section
P.O. Box 70
108 Cherry Street
Burlington, VT 05402-0070

Virginia Division of Vital Records
P.O. Box 1000
Richmond, VA 23218-1000

Washington Department of Health
Center for Health Statistics
P.O. Box 9709
Olympia, WA 98507-9709

West Virginia Vital Registration Office
Room 165
350 Capitol Street
Charleston, WV 25301-3701

Wisconsin Vital Records Office
1 West Wilson Street
P.O. Box 309
Madison, WI 53701-0309

Wyoming Vital Records Services
Hathaway Building
Cheyenne, WY 820

State Archives

Alabama Department of Archives & History
624 Washington Avenue
Montgomery, Alabama 36130-0100
Phone: 334-242-4435
Fax: 334-240-3433
www.archives.state.al.us

Alaska State Archives
PO Box 110525
141 Willoughby Avenue
Juneau, AK 99811-0525
Phone: 907-465-2270
Fax: 907-465-2465
www.archives.state.ak.us

Arizona Archives Division
1901 W. Madison Street
Phoenix, AZ 85009
Phone: 602-542-4159
Fax: 602-542-4402
www.lib.az.us/archives/index.cfm

Arkansas History Commission
One Capitol Mall
Little Rock, AR 77201
Phone: 501-682-6900
www.ark-ives.com

SW Arkansas Regional Archives
201 Highway 195 South
Washington, Arkansas 71862
Phone: 870-983-2633
Fax: 870-983-2636
www.southwestarchives.com

California State Archives
1020 "O" Street
Sacramento, CA 95814
Phone: 916-653-2246
Fax: 916-653-7363
www.sos.ca.gov/archives

Colorado State Archives
1313 Sherman, Room 1B20
Denver, CO 80203
Phone: 303-866-2358
Fax: 303866-2257
www.colorado.gov/dpa/doit/archives/

Connecticut State Archives
231 Capitol Avenue
Hartford, CT 06106
Phone: 860-757-6580
Archives Staff: 860-757-6595
Fax: 860-757-6542
www.cslib.org/archives/

Delaware Public Archives
121 Duke of York Street,
Dover, DE 19901
Phone: 302-744-5000
Fax: 302-739-6710
archives.delaware.gov/

Florida State Archives
R.A. Gray Building
500 South Bronough Street
Tallahassee, FL 32399-0250
Phone: 850-245-6700
Fax: 850-488-4894
dlis.dos.state.fl.us/index_researchers.cfm

Georgia Archives
5800 Jonesboro Road
Morrow, GA 30260
Phone: 678-364-3700
Fax: 678-364-3856
sos.georgia.gov/archives/

Hawaii Historic Records Branch
Kekauluohi Building,
Iolani Palace Grounds
Honolulu, HI 96813
Phone: 808-586-0329
Fax: 808-586-0330
www.state.hi.us/dags/archives/

Idaho State Historical Society Library & Archives
Public Archives and Research Library
2205 Old Penitentiary Road
Boise, ID 83712
Phone: 208-334-2620
Fax: 208-334-3198
www.idahohistory.net/library_archives.html

Illinois State Archives
Margaret Cross Norton Building
Capitol Complex
Springfield, IL 62756
Telephone: 217782-4682
Fax: 217524-3930
www.cyberdriveillinois.com/departments/archives/archives.html

Indiana State Archives
6440 East 30th Street
Indianapolis, Indiana 46219
Phone: 317-591-5222
Fax: 317-591-5324
www.in.gov/icpr/2436.htm

Iowa State Library of Iowa
Ola Babcock Miller Building
1112 E. Grand Ave.,
Des Moines, IA 50319-0233
Phone: 515-281-4105
Fax: 515-281-6191
Electronic Depository website:
publications.iowa.gov/
www.statelibraryofiowa.org/

Kansas State Historical Society
6425 Southwest Sixth Avenue
Topeka, KS 66615
Phone: 785-272-8681 ext. 117
Fax: 785-272-8682
www.kshs.org/genealogists/index.htm

Kentucky Department for Libraries & Archives
300 Coffee Tree Road
Frankfort, Kentucky 40601
Mailing Address
P.O. Box 537
Frankfort, KY 40602
Phone: 502-564-8300
Fax: 502-564-5773
www.kdla.ky.gov/

Louisiana State Archives
3851 Essen Lane
Baton Rouge, LA 70809
Phone: 225-922-1000
Fax: 225-922-0433
www.sos.louisiana.gov/tabid/53/Default.aspx

Maine State Archives
84 State House Station
Augusta, ME 04333-0084
Phone: 207287-5788
Fax: 207287-5739
www.state.me.us/sos/arc/

Maryland State Archives
350 Rowe Boulevard
Annapolis, MD 21401
Phone: 410-260-6400
Fax: 410-974-2525
www.msa.md.gov/

Massachusetts Archives
Secretary of Commonwealth
Massachusetts Archives
220 Morrissey Boulevard
Boston, MA 02125
Phone: 617-727-2816 Fax: 617-288-8429

Michigan Archives
Michigan Historical Center
702 West Kalamazoo Street
P.O. Box 30740
Lansing, MI 48909-8240
Phone: 517-373-1408
Fax: 517-241-1658
www.michigan.gov/hal/0,1607,7-160-21859---C,00.html

Minnesota State Archives
Minnesota Historical Society
345 Kellogg Boulevard West
St. Paul, MN 55102-1906
Phone: 651-259-3260
Fax: 651-296-9961
www.mnhs.org/preserve/records/index.htm

Mississippi Department of Archives
200 North St.
Jackson, MS 39201
Mailing Address
P.O. Box 571
Jackson, MS 39205-0571
Phone: 601-576-6876
Fax: 601-576-6964
www.mdah.state.ms.us/admin/contact.html

Missouri State Archives
600 W. Main
P.O. Box 1747
Jefferson City, MO 65102
Phone: 573-751-3280
Fax: 573-526-7333
www.sos.mo.gov/archives/

Montana Historical Society
P.O. Box 201201
225 North Roberts Street
Helena, MT 59620
Phone: 406-444-2694
Fax: 406-444-2696
www.his.state.mt.us/

Nebraska Library/Archives Division
1500 R Street
P.O. Box 82554
Lincoln, NE 68501
Phone: 402-471-4751
Fax: 402471-3100

Nevada State Library & Archives
100 North Stewart Street
Carson City, NV 89701
Phone: 775-684-3310
Fax: 775-684-3311
dmla.clan.lib.nv.us/docs/nsla/archives/

New Hampshire Archives
71 South Fruit Street
Concord, NH 03301
Phone: 603-271-2236
Fax: 603-271-2272
www.sos.nh.gov/archives/

New Mexico State Archives
1205 Camino Carlos Rey
Santa Fe, NM 87507
Phone: 505-476-7903
Fax: 505-476-7910
www.nmcpr.state.nm.us/

New Jersey Public Records & Archives
225 West State Street-Level 2
P.O. Box 307
Trenton, NJ 08625-0307
Phone: 609-292-6260
Fax: 609-396-2454
www.state.nj.us/state/darm/

New York State Archives
New York State Education Department
Cultural Education Center
Albany, NY 12230
Phone: 518-474-8955
www.archives.nysed.gov/aindex.shtml

North Carolina State Archives
109 E. Jones St.
Raleigh, N.C. 27601
Mailing address
4614 Mail Service Center
Raleigh, NC 27699-4614
Phone: 919-807-7310
Fax: 919-733-1354
www.ah.dcr.state.nc.us/archives/

North Dakota State Archives
612 East Boulevard Avenue
Bismarck, ND 58505-0830
Phone: 701328-2091
Fax: 701328-2650
www.nd.gov/hist/sal.htm

Ohio Historical Society Archives
Research Services Department
1982 Velma Avenue
Columbus, OH 43211
Phone: 614-297-2510
www.ohiohistory.org/resource/statearc

Oklahoma State Archives
200 Northeast Eighteenth Street
Oklahoma City, OK 73105-3298
Phone: 405-521-2502
Fax: 405-525-7804
www.odl.state.ok.us/oar/

Oregon State Archives
800 Summer St. NE
Salem, OR 97310
Phone: 503-373-0701
Fax: 503-373-0953
arcweb.sos.state.or.us/

Pennsylvania State Archives
350 North Street
Harrisburg, PA 17120-0090
Phone: 717-783-3281
www.phmc.state.pa.us/bah/dam/overview.htm

Rhode Island State Archives
337 Westminster Street
Providence, RI 02903
Phone: 401-222-2353
Fax: 401-222-3199
www.sec.state.ri.us/Archives/

South Carolina State Archives
8301 Parklane Road
Columbia, SC 29223
Phone: 803-896-6100
Fax: 803-896-6198
scdah.sc.gov

South Dakota State Archives
900 Governors Drive
Pierre, SD 57501-2217
Phone: 605-773-3804
Fax: 605-773-6041
www.sdhistory.org/arc/archives.htm

Tennessee State Library & Archives
403 Seventh Avenue North
Nashville, TN 37243-0312
Phone: 615-741-2764
Fax: 615-532-2472
www.tennessee.gov/tsla

Texas State Library & Archives
1201 Brazos
P.O. Box 12927
Austin, TX 78711-2927
Main Phone: 512-463-5455
Phone: 512-463-5480
www.tsl.state.tx.us/

Utah State Archives
346 S Rio Grande St
Salt Lake City, UT 84101-1106
Main Number: 801531-3848
Fax: 801531-3854
www.archives.state.ut.us/main/

Vermont State Archives
Office of the Secretary of State
26 Terrace Street
Montpelier, VT 05609-1101
Phone: 802-828-2308
Fax: 802-828-1135
vermont-archives.org/

Virginia Archives Research Services
Library of Virginia
800 East Broad Street
Richmond, VA 23219-8000
Phone: 804-692-3888
Fax: 804-692-3556
www.lva.lib.va.us/

Washington State Archives
Archives and Records Building
1129 Washington Street SE
P.O. Box 40238
Olympia, WA 98504-0238
Phone: 360-586-1492
www.secstate.wa.gov/archives/Default.aspx

West Virginia State Archives
Archives & History Library
The Cultural Center
1900 Kanawha Boulevard East
Charleston, WV 25305-0300
Phone: 304-558-0230
www.wvculture.org/history/wvsamenu.html

Wisconsin State Historical Society
Archives Reference
816 State Street
Madison, WI 53706-1417
Phone: 608-264-6460 Fax: 608-264-6472
wisconsinhistory.org/libraryarchives/

Wyoming State Archives
Barrett Building
2301 Central Avenue
Cheyenne, WY 82002
Phone: 307-777-7826 Fax: 307-777-7044
wyoarchives.state.wy.us/index.htm

Adoption Websites

ADOPTION RELATED SITES FOR BIRTH FAMILIES

- About Adoption: www.adoption.about.com
- Adopt Assistance Information Support: www.reunite.com
- Adoption Assist: www.adoption-assist.com /pands/search.html
- Adoption Crossroads: www.adoptioncrossroads.org
- Adoption.com: www.adoption.com
- Adoption.org: www.adoption.org
- Adoptee's Post & Search Page: www.members.aol.com/ceeart/index16.html
- Adoption Triad Outreach: www.adoptiontriad.org/registry.htm
- Alumni: www.alumni.net
- Ancestry: www.ancestry.com
- Bastard Nation: www.bastards.org
- BestLinks: www.geocities.com/Heartland/1637
- BirthMoms: www.bmom.net
- Birthday List - Search: www.cs.vu.nl/~michel/birthday/birthdate/birthdate .9.html
- Cemetery Records: www.interment.net
- Census Bureau: www.census.gov
- Cherokee: www.powersource.com/cherokee
- Dawn's Birthmother/Adoption Resources: www.members.tripod.com/~HevensDawn/adoption.html
- Family Birth Records: www.familybirthrecords.com
- Family Ties Adoption Search Database: www.geocities.com/Heartland/Ranch/1049/index.html
- Finding parents' names with newspapers: www.genealogy.com/00000545.html
- Free Missing Person Searches: www.findmissingpeople.com/freesearch.html
- Janet's Adoption Links: www. members.tripod.com/~gene_pool/2ado.htm

- jlight's Adoption Search Links:
www.members.tripod.com/~jlightkeeper/adoption.html
- Kindred Pursuits - Registry for Canada and USA:
www.kindredpursuits.org
- Lynch's Adoption Reunion Registry:
www.geocities.com/heartland/acres/9942/registry.html
- Lynch's Maiden Name Registry:
www.lynch.bizland.com/maidennameregistry.html

BLACK MARKET REGISTRIES, Etc.

- A Black Market Adoptee Searching For Birthfamily:
www.geocities.com/Heartland/Garden/1903/index.html
- A Cole Baby's Home Away From Home:
www.afn.org/~w4gj
- Article: Black Market Adoption Information Guide:
www.angelfire.com/fl2/colebaby/story.html
- Adoptions Handled by Bessie Bernard & Irwin Slater:
www.geocities.com/Heartland/Lake/5803/bessie.html
- Black Market Adoption Support List:
www.onelist.com/subscribe.cgi/Blackmarketbabies
- Learn More About Cole Babies: www.afn.org/~w4gj/COLE.html
- Guitbowl's Home Page:
www.hometown.aol.com/Guitbowl/index.html
- Hightower Black Market Babies Of Texarkana,
Texas: www.vickishome.com/adoption
- Ideal Maternity Home: Butterbox Babies' Home
Page: www3.ns.sympatico.ca/bhartlen
- Registry Page:
www.angelfire.com/fl2/colebaby/registry.html
- Silent Legacy: The Hicks Clinic Birth Registry
(McCaysville, Georgia): www.hicksclinic.com
- Tennessee Black Market Adoption Information:
www.geocities.com/Heartland/Bluffs/3592/TNBMA
- The Cole Babies' Story:
www.geocities.com/Heartland/Lake/5803/colebaby
- Home of the Butterbox Babies (Nova Scotia):
www3.ns.sympatico.ca/bhartlen
- The Veil Hospital Information:
www.geocities.com/Heartland/Garden/2313/veilnursery
- The Willows Maternity Home:
www.geocities.com/Heartland/Garden/2313/thewillows

- Twins Separated At Birth: Nebraska: www.members.aol.com/ceeart/index.html
- You Are Here: Black Market Resource Page: www.maxpages.com/tabu70/Home

MISCELLANEOUS RESOURCES

- Commonbond: www.angelfire.com/fl/commonbond/index.html
- Find A Doctor: www.doctor.webmd.com /physician_finder/home.aspx?sponsor=core
- Florida Online Family Finders: www.geocities.com/Heartland/Woods/2677
- Florida, Citrus County Official Records Search: www.clerk.citrus.fl.us
- Florida, Leon County Marriage Records Online: www.clerk.leon.fl.us
- Georgia Adoption Reunion Registry: www.adoptions.dhr.state.ga.us/reunion.htm
- N. Georgia Reunion Registry: www.geocities.com/Heartland/Bluffs/3592/GA
- Illinois Adoption Registry: www.macadopt.org/main.htm
- Illinois, Midwest Adoption Center: www.macadopt.org/main.htm
- Institutions for the developmentally disabled:
- Hospital Locator: www.helplinedatabase.com/hospital-us/
- Indiana Searching: www.geocities.com/Heartland/Park/3560
- Birth Records, Miami County, Kansas: skyways.lib.ks.us/genweb/miami/birth
- Ole Kentucky Home Registry: www.geocities.com/Heartland/Bluffs/3592/KY
- Kentucky Adoption Reunion Registry: www.kyadoptions.com
- Louisana, Seller's Baptist Home Mailing List: www.members.aol.com/CEdwa49620/sbch.html
- Louisiana Adoption Database: www.angelfire.com/la2/adoption/page16.htm
- The Maine Registry: www.angelfire.com/me2/themaineregistry/index.html
- Seeker Radio Show: www.the-seeker.com/radio.htm

- Maternity Home Registry, Kayhh's: www.geocities.com/Heartland/8529/adopt/1MHreg
- Maryland's Mutual Consent Voluntary Adoption Registry: www.dhr.state.md.us/voladopr.htm
- Metro Reunion Registry: www.metroreunionregistry.org
- Massachusetts Registry: www.members.aol.com/Espaura/MAadopt.html
- Michigan Listing: www.geocities.com/heartland/7233
- Minnesota Fathers' Adoption Registry: www.health.state.mn.us/divs/chs/registry/resourc.htm
- Mississippi Reunion Registry: www.geocities.com/Heartland/Bluffs/3592/MS
- NH Adoption Registry: www.angelfire.com/nh/redmomma/index.html
- New Jersey, OASIS: members.tripod.com/BastardGoddess/OASIS.html
- Sylvia's New York Adoption Page: www.nyadoption.org
- Oregon Adoption Search Information & Registry: www.barysoftware.com
- Rhode Island Adoption Registry: www.angelfire.com/nh/redmomma/index.html
- Risk Factors in Children Adopted from the Former Soviet Union: www.adoption-research.org/parent.html
- Tennessee Reunion Registry: www.geocities.com/Heartland/Bluffs/3592
- Tennessee Adoption Registry: www.geocities.com/Heartland/Flats/9073
- Texas Edna Gladney Reunion Registry: www.geocities.com/voasearch/gladney
- Vermont Adoption Registry: www.angelfire.com/nh/redmomma/index.html
- Virginia Adoption Registry: www.geocities.com/Heartland/Plains/6436
- Metro Reunion Registry: www.metroreunionregistry.org
- Washington D. C. Metro Reunion Registry: www.metroreunionregistry.org
- I.C.A.R.E.'s Wisconsin Adoptee/Birth Family Registry: www.emerald.jvlnet.com/~icare

Index

Other media by Crary Publications.

Child I Cannot Claim CD
Written by a first mother to the
daughter she was forced to relinquish
and is sung by a first sister

A Romantic Historical
Adventure

How to Protect Your Small
Business Against Fraud,
Debtors, Theft, Workplace
Violence and more!

Give the Gift of ADOPTION RECORDS HANDBOOK
To your friends or family who may want to start searching.

YES, I want _____ copies of *Adoption Records Handbook* for $14.95 each within the USA. International Orders are $25.00 each.

Child I Cannot Claim CD is $3.95; *Business Security* book is $19.95; *My Father's Daughter* is $15.95. Books as seen at: www.CraryPublications.com

My check or money order for $_____ is enclosed. International orders must be accompanied by a postal money order in U.S. funds.

Please Print Plainly:

_____

Name

_____

Street Address

_____

City/State/Zip

_____

Phone

_____

E-Mail

_____

Item Ordering

Mail to:
Crary Publications
405 Lehman Street
Las Vegas, NV 89110

Credit Card ordering of books can be done online through PayPal under the account of PayPal@AdoptionRecords.com, through Amazon.com, BarnesandNoble.com or ordered from your local bookstore or library.

LaVergne, TN USA
07 January 2010
169180LV00001B/24/P